STAINING
AND
POLISHING

INCLUDING VARNISHING & OTHER
METHODS OF FINISHING WOOD,
WITH APPENDIX OF RECIPES

First Edition	.	. *November, 1917*
Second Edition	.	. *May, 1918*
Third Edition	.	. *October, 1919*
Fourth Edition	.	. *March, 1920*
Fifth Edition	.	. *November, 1921*
Sixth Edition	.	. *October, 1923*
Seventh Edition	.	. *June, 1925*
Eighth Edition	.	. *February, 1926*
Ninth Edition		. *September, 1927*

LONDON
EVANS BROTHERS, LIMITED
MONTAGUE HOUSE, RUSSELL SQUARE, W.C.1

FOREWORD

THE aim of this Volume is three-fold. In the first place, the intention is to place before the reader full information in regard to practically every method of wood finishing. In doing this the best known workshop practices have been followed. No good process, however old, has been ignored; at the same time, more recent methods current in present-day polishing shops and adopted by expert craftsmen have been included.

A second aim is to emphasise, not only that woodworking and wood finishing are branches of one craft, but that thought and workmanship are inseparable. Staining and polishing may not be classed among the fine arts, but they are crafts in which the highest degree of skill can be attained. The man who puts thought and artistic feeling into his work is insensible to any dreariness of routine. He realises what quality in workmanship means. Thought may be traced through every movement of his polishing rubber, and for himself he sets a standard which he studiously endeavours to reach.

And another aim of the Volume is to suggest polishing (with its kindred methods of finishing wood) as an interesting and well-paid craft for many who might otherwise drift into less skilled and less lucrative occupations. In itself it is a craft of engrossing and developing interest, one in which new ideas will constantly occur to the intelligent and inventive mind, and thus one in which the best men can always rise to good positions.

J. C. S. BROUGH.

CONTENTS

	PAGE
STAINS FOR WOODS	1

Water Stains—Oil Stains—Varnish Stains.

WOODS FOR STAINING 9

Characteristics of Woods—Preparing the Wood—Fillers.

STAINING 15

Applying the Stain—Colour Chart—Colour Schemes and Operations—Impregnated Wood—Ebonising—Staining Wicker-work—Dyeing Woods.

STAINING 31

Treatment of various Woods.

FRENCH POLISHING 39

Shellac—The Polishing Workshop and Equipment—The Polishing Rubber.

PREPARING FURNITURE FOR FRENCH POLISHING 49

Preparing Surfaces—Preparing New Wood—Wax Stopping—Fillers and Filling.

FRENCH POLISHING 61

Fatting or Bodying-in—Bodying-up or Working-up—Colouring—Spiriting—Supporting Work.

GLAZING, ETC. 77

Glazing—Dry-shining—Egg-shell and Dull Polishing—Spirit Enamelling—Treatment of Carved Work.

MATCHING AND IMPROVING 87

Removing old Polish—Re-polishing old Furniture.

CONTENTS (*Continued*).

	PAGE
DEFECTS IN POLISHING AND THEIR REMEDIES	101

Sweating — Cracks — Bruises — Blisters — Dulness — Finger-marks — Fading — Scratches — Whiteness—Patchiness—Stains.

POLISHING INLAID WORK, ETC. . . . 113

Inlaid Work — Marquetry Transfers — Polishing Turned Work—Polishing Fretwork.

OAK AND ITS VARIOUS FINISHES . . . 125

Fuming — Dark and Antique Oak — Green and Grey Oak—Polishing Oak Coffins—Bleached Oak.

OIL-POLISHING AND WAX-POLISHING . . 133

Oil-polishing Furniture — Floors — Wax-polishing Furniture and Floors.

STENCILLING ON WOOD AND ORNAMENTAL WOOD STAINING 143

VARNISH 151

The Uses of Varnish—Making Varnish—Classes of Varnish.

VARNISHING. 161

Surfaces for Varnishing—Brushes, etc.—Applying Varnish—Felting Down—Spirit Varnishing, etc.

FAULTS IN VARNISHING 175

Their Remedies—Testing Varnishes—General Hints on Varnishing.

APPENDIX 183

Recipes for Stains—Water Coating—Self Colours—Polishes — Revivers — Fillers, Varnishes, etc.

INDEX 199

STAINS FOR WOODS

WATER STAINS—OIL STAINS—VARNISH STAINS

A GOOD craftsman should be able not only to execute an elaborate piece of work, but also to give the article a properly finished appearance. In the furnishing trade, the cabinet-maker, the upholsterer and the polisher are distinct persons, each being often quite unfamiliar with any branch of the business beyond his own special one. But is there any sound reason for this being the case? The furniture trade artisan who is able to do polishing and all that appertains to it will command a better market for his labour than he who ignores everything outside his own particular groove.

It is well, too, for the woodworker—whether amateur or professional—to know something of the art of staining, as it is quite possible by this means to make a handsome suite of furniture from common wood, where the expense would put oak, mahogany or walnut out of reach.

What Staining Is.—Broadly speaking, staining may be sufficiently defined as the saturation of a porous material with a colouring solution. It might be considered as a secondary kind of painting, but should be distinguished from graining; for, whilst in the latter the original wood is entirely ignored, and a new surface produced on which the colour and veining of another wood is imitated, in staining the general appearance of the original wood is retained, as regards grain, etc., though the colour is made different from the natural one. The process of staining consists, in the main, of laying on the stains in the form of mere washes, so as to change the shade of the wood to a darker or warmer colour, or to make a wood which, in its natural grain, resembles another, correspond in colour with the latter.

The Aim of Staining is, in the first place, to colour the fibre in an agreeable manner, and in the second place

Staining and Polishing

not only to maintain the natural beauty of the grain, but also to throw into relief the different degrees of light and shade which the grain presents.

As regards the colouring, the whole matter depends upon the selective or absorptive capacity of the different portions of the wood for the various dyes used in the staining process. Certain portions of the wood absorb a greater portion of the dye (relatively to their area) than other portions, the result being that without any manipulation on the part of the operator different tones of colour are obtained. The choice of colours or dyes is of importance, and offers a wide field for originality and artistic skill. The whole question, indeed, of the treatment of woodwork so as to leave it in its natural state is an extremely interesting one, and has not by any means been studied in this country with that degree of interest which it merits.

THE VARIOUS STAINS.

The Stains used in rendering to inferior woods the appearance of those of better quality are usually of a fairly powerful kind; that is to say, they are capable of producing on the surface of the work a good depth of colour, thus hiding in a measure the true nature of the wood. Those experienced in detecting stained work know that by the exercise of skill the colours of wood can be exactly imitated, but not so the grain, or the tiny fissures on the surface of most kinds of wood. However expert the polisher may be, he cannot render, say, to American white-wood the open grain of oak, and the worker who desires to " see through " the polish must acquaint himself with woods as they are in their natural state. With regard to the different kinds of stain in general use, we can now proceed to a description of their constituents.

The Various Classes of Staining are known by the names of water staining, oil staining, varnish staining, spirit staining, chemical staining, wax staining, and water

Stains for Woods

coating. Other processes worthy of note are : Colouring, improving, grain imitation, etc. These latter, however, will be dealt with in the section on French Polishing and subsequent chapters.

The two principal classes are "water" and "spirit," the names denoting the medium used for dissolving the dyes of which they are made. Both kinds of stain are obtainable ready mixed from suppliers of polish in all the necessary colours, which include oak, walnut, mahogany, rosewood, ebony, art green, etc., and where quantities of stain are required and uniformity of colour is desired, so that the material can be depended upon to always give the same results, the worker will do well to purchase the ready-made article in preference to mixing his own. By many, of course, it is often found that stains in powdered form, which require but the addition of methylated spirit or water, are very useful; and more especially is this the case where the polishing has to be done away from home or the workshop.

Generally speaking, spirit stains are superior in effect to those mixed with water, as the spirit, being volatile, dries off quickly, while with water stains the grain of the wood has a tendency to rise, which is accentuated by their comparative slowness in drying. Again, spirit stains can be successfully applied to woodwork which has been previously polished, and from the surface of which the old polish has not been entirely removed, while in using water stains it is imperative that neither polish nor oil be present, as water will not penetrate either of these.

In Water Staining only such substances as are soluble in water and have no body in them are used. These include gamboge, indigo, logwood, the juice of berries and barks of trees, as well as other substances of a more earthy nature. The colours used in oil staining must also be of a transparent nature and similar to those pigments used for water staining, except that they are ground in oil instead of water. The siennas, umbers, lakes, etc., belong to this

Staining and Polishing

class. Sometimes linseed oil alone is used, but this changes the colour of the wood very little. Varnish staining is nothing more or less than the addition of varnish to the oil stains. This is, however, done for a specific purpose, being sometimes used to check the absorption of the wood, or to procure a better surface for either varnishing or polishing.

Water Coating is the use of body colours ground in water, as ochre, umber, Venetian red, chrome, drop-black, etc. It is, in reality, a form of distempering, differing, however, in the fact that it is not all left on the wood to dry. Size is added to bind the colour, as in distempering. This process, of course, hides the natural grain of the wood and disguises its shortcomings and defects. The various processes connected with the application of these classes of staining will be fully dealt with in their proper places.

In Spirit Staining certain dyes are used which are more tractable or more easily miscible in spirit than in the other mediums, and hence are used in spirit. In other respects this kind of staining does not differ largely from that known as oil staining. Chemical staining is the use of aqueous solutions not in themselves having colour, but which change the colour of the woods to which they are applied, as soda, lime, potash, ammonia, and various sulphates and salts.

Wax Stains.—Oak and other hard woods are often wax stained and polished by hand. Wax stains are made from a mixture of beeswax and turpentine, and stained with oil colours, like vandyke brown, burnt and raw siennas, etc. They are applied freely when warm, and when soaked in and hardened (say, after about a day or so) a fine dull egg-shell polish is produced by briskly rubbing with a hard brush or rough piece of jute canvas.

Oil Stains are the most durable amongst the various classes of staining, and the oil, by reason of its slowness in drying, penetrates far into the wood. Any kind of finish is suitable over an oil stain. Turpentine stains are valuable

Stains for Woods

for soft woods, as they show less tendency to roughen the wood at the soft year-ring marks than water stains do. They, however, dry rapidly, much as an ordinary spirit stain does. It may be well to mention here that a wax-polished finish should not be adopted when a turps stain has been employed, as the turpentine in the wood would dissolve the wax and cause spots. An ordinary polish or varnish can be used with safety.

Water Stains.—As their name implies, water stains have water as a vehicle, and they are not, generally speaking, so powerful as spirit stains. Heavy staining often requires a number of applications of the solution to the work and, the grain of the wood having a tendency to swell, it is necessary, in using water stains especially, to carefully glass-paper the wood between each coat of stain—care, of course, being taken that as little of the colouring be removed during the process of papering as possible. Water dries but slowly, and its evaporation must not be hastened by artificial means; and, although more costly, spirit stains, which are volatile (*i.e.*, have quick vaporising powers), are less liable to raise the grain of the wood, the moisture remaining upon the surface a comparatively short time only. Where only a light stain is to be applied, the work may be damped off first and the grain so raised papered off when dry. On the stain being subsequently applied, considerably less rubbing down will be required, and consequently fewer coats of stains.

The Cheapest Kinds of stain are those made of size, painters' dry colours, and water, the first-named ingredient being used as a binding agent to prevent the stain brushing off. In reality, these stains are not suited to what may be termed a legitimate French-polished finish, but rather to use in connection with varnish, which, if desired, may subsequently be subjected to finishing with the polish rubber.

To make a stain of this variety the quantity of size to be added to each gallon of water may be taken as 2 lbs.

Staining and Polishing

but exact proportions are not material, provided that when the stain is dry it does not rub off. The stains are made and also applied hot, a moderately soft brush—a painter's sash-tool is the kind required—being used to put them on. Regarding the quantity of colour to be added to the size and water, this depends upon the depth of tone required and on the colouring power of the powder.

The most popular stains are undoubtedly those which have water as a medium, they being the cheapest and the easiest to make. Like the spirit stains, they dry quickly on new wood; but, whereas the latter will evaporate quickly on any surface, water stains are not as quick on a non-porous surface (such as old polish or varnish) as they are on a porous one. The great drawback of water stains when used on new work is that they have a tendency to roughen the surface and raise the grain of the wood. This is more in evidence when coarse glass-paper has been employed in cleaning up the wood. When it does occur, the evil may be mitigated by cutting down the grain with fine glass-paper whilst the wood is still damp. The fibres of the wood which swelled by damp or moisture are thereby partly forced back again into the pores. Some woods require this treatment several times before they cease to come up rough. Afterwards, apply the stain less liberally than before. The beauty of water stains is enhanced by the resinous portions of the grain resisting the action of the water, and thus showing up brighter and in clear contrast to the spongy or absorbent portion of the grain.

Although an appendix of recipes is given at the end of this volume, it is desirable here to give a list of stains which may be used for the different classes mentioned.

Water Stains.—Vandyke brown, raw umber, burnt umber, raw sienna, burnt sienna, blue black, indigo, mahogany lake, yellow lake, gamboge, terra vert, aniline dyes, alkaline dyes, and other transparent or partially transparent pigments; also Manders', Stephens', and Johnson's prepared stains.

Stains for Woods

Oil Stains.—All the pigments named above, and any others that are transparent, but they must be ground in oil, whereas the above are ground in water ; also japanners' black thinned with turpentine, and asphaltum thinned with turpentine.

Varnish Stain.—As stated previously, this is simply the addition of varnish to the oil stains. There are many prepared varnish stains on the market.

Spirit Stains.—Boiled and macerated solutions of the various dyewoods and dyestuffs : as logwood, sanders' wood, Brazilian redwood, aniline powders, dragon's blood, turmeric, arsenate of copper, saffron, indigo and others. Also various berries, cochineal, etc.

Chemical Stains.—Alkaline manganates, permanganate of potash, Epsom salts, ammonia, carbonate of soda, bichromate of potash, acetic acid, pearlash, Roman vitriol, nitric acid, picric acid, common salt, subacetate of copper, sulphate of iron, and other substances.

Water Coating.—Ochres, umbers, Venetian red, lamp black, rose pink, etc., all in size.

Wax Stains.—Best beeswax, dissolved in turpentine and stained with oil colours.

Stephens' stains are admirable, and to these may be added the numerous aniline dyes, which are divided into two classes, the alkaline and the acid, and these must not be mixed together. One dissolves in water, the other in spirits. There are a great number of different coloured stains of this character on the market. Most druggists sell aniline dyes in packets and in tubes, and these may be usefully employed on wood for self-colours only, as distinct from various imitations of woods. Many dyes and colours are to be obtained from common plants growing in abundance almost everywhere. There are also patent stains now on the market which are both a preservative and a stain. They claim to protect wood from dry rot, or any

Staining and Polishing

other form of decay. They are also stated to be verminproof. They are made in various shades, notably greens and browns, as well as in black.

Numerous paint and varnish manufacturing firms make stains in various colours, usually representative of the more popular woods, such as mahogany, walnut, oak, rosewood, satinwood, ebony, maple, etc.

The stains here referred to are pure stains or dyes which need to be afterwards either varnished or polished. Invariably the makers recommend sizing after staining and prior to varnishing—one coat of size for a French-polished finish, and two coats for a varnished finish. They also supply both the size and varnish required.

The so-called varnish stains do not penetrate the wood, but simply lie on the surface as a thick, semi-transparent lacquer. The beauty of a stain consists chiefly in its penetrating quality. These stains have the advantage, however, of enabling a hurried job to be done quickly, and they are all right for cheap work; but if one wishes to make a perfect job he is not recommended to use varnish stains. Unlike pure stains, these can be procured anywhere, the makers of this class of stains being legion.

WOODS FOR STAINING

CHARACTERISTICS OF WOODS   PREPARING THE WOOD
FILLERS

IN cabinet-making chiefly hard woods are used. For wood-carving, fretwork, etc., softer woods are occasionally employed, and when work is veneered a soft wood is sometimes used underneath.

Light-coloured woods are of course the best for staining. They include light oak, ash, holly, sycamore, maple, Canadian pine, canary wood, white chestnut, satinwood, beech, American birch, lime, boxwood, pear, yellow pine, pitch pine, poplar, etc. In case the reader gets confused among the different names employed for certain woods, it will be as well to state that many of the variously-named American pines, etc., are but different names adopted in different localities for one and the same kind of wood. The same remarks apply to Northern pine, red fir, yellow fir, Scotch fir, and yellow deal; also to white fir, spruce, whitewood, and white deal. Both hard and soft woods may be stained, though perhaps the latter class are more used for this purpose, embracing the cheaper woods which invariably are used to imitate the more expensive ones, the latter usually belonging to the hard-wood class. Below is a list of hard and soft woods which, although not botanically correct, may be taken as a reference for staining purposes.

Hard Woods.—Beech, boxwood, amboyna, Spanish mahogany, birch, ash, cherry, ebony, jasper, maple, oak, olive, orange, pear, apple, greenheart, pitch pine, rosewood, satinwood, teak, tiger-wood, zebra, thuya-wood, kauri-pine, etc.

Soft Woods.—Yellow pine, white fir, Italian walnut, lime, Canadian pine, cedar, white chestnut, plane, lacewood, poplar, satin-walnut, sequoia or Californian red wood, etc.

Staining and Polishing

Useful Woods.—American whitewood is the wood which most readily lends itself to staining by the use of aniline dyes, as it is freer from knots than most others. Next to it would perhaps be cottonwood or basswood. These woods are very similar in character, of a yellowish colour, and are excellent for imitating either mahogany or walnut ; they are undoubtedly the best substitutes for mahogany. Birch is also often used to represent mahogany. A good hard white wood like beech is also valuable for staining in imitation of mahogany. Pine or deal is a good wood to use for staining in imitation of plain walnut. The pine grain shows under a suitable stain the dark characteristics of the walnut wood. Figured mahogany or birch can be made to closely imitate rosewood by the use of a suitable stain, while yellow pine, simply varnished with one or two coats, will be as near the tone of maple as can be got without painting and graining.

For the imitation of ebony, the following woods are all good to stain :—Plane, chestnut, sycamore, holly, cherry, apple, pear, and hazelwood. The four latter are the best for this purpose, as their grain and general appearance when stained black exhibit the most complete imitation of natural ebony. Holly, however, forms an excellent substitute when stained black, the bluish-grey variety, termed dark holly, being chiefly recommended for this class of work. Sometimes oak is dyed to resemble ebony, but we think this is of rare occurrence. It may be mentioned that pine is not a good wood to ebonise. The operation of fuming is usually restricted to two woods—oak and mahogany. Sycamore and beech are excellent woods for both dyeing and staining, but for the latter holly is superior to sycamore. The French dyed veneers are mostly of sycamore.

PREPARING THE WOOD.

It is essential to success in staining that the wood be nice and smooth, free from grease or dirt marks, and that

Woods for Staining

it contains as few knots as possible. Large knots are unsightly, and unless very small and but slightly developed they should be cut out, another piece of the same kind of wood being let in as neatly as possible.

Glass-papering.—If the wood feels rough when passed over with the hand, it should be given a slight rub with glass-paper, using No. 0. This should be held quite flat against the wood and rubbed evenly up and down with as long sweeps as possible, taking care to rub the same way as the grain. If the paper happens to be rubbed across the grain, such parts when stained will turn out darker than the rest. The corners of panels should be well got into, and to ensure success in this direction a perfectly square piece of cork or wood should be employed. The glass-paper should be wrapped right round the cork, and to prevent it slipping may be fastened down by either gum, paste, or tacks. To obviate the risk of scratching, the wood should be thoroughly dusted previous to rubbing.

Grease Marks.—If the wood happens to have some dirty marks, these may be removed with the glass-paper, though care must be taken not to abrade the surface by undue pressure at such parts. If this fails, try rubbing the marks with a linen rag dipped in turpentine or benzine, the latter for preference. When the marks are of a sooty character, use soapy water, sponging over afterwards with clean cold water, and allowing sufficient time to dry before anything further is done to the work. Sometimes the finished work turns out "spotty." This is due to the presence of oil or grease on the surface of the wood prior to staining, or possibly to portions of glue which have not been cleaned off when fixing. These spots will turn out lighter than the stain, to the complete detriment of the finished work. To remedy these rub well with benzine, and finish off with a rag dipped in fine whiting. The glue must of course be scraped off.

Staining and Polishing

Dressing.—If the wood should happen to be of poor quality or badly dressed, it would be advisable to adopt some means of making an even surface as regards suction so that the stain will appear of an uniform tint when applied. To obtain this result, any of the undermentioned materials may be used, though for most cases the first-named is the best:—

Glue Size.—This is cheap, easily made and applied, and may be safely used in all such instances as these. It can be obtained anywhere, but the strength varies according to the make. Cannon's size is a good make, and is put up in ¼-lb. packets. The size must not be used too strong, or it may cause the finishing coats to crack. A fair medium is in the proportion of from 1½ to 2½ gallons of water to the pound of dry size. The exact strength of the mixture is determined by the condition of the wood. If it be very open in texture, or of a very spongy nature, then the size must be used fairly strong; but unless this is the case the size must only be used weak. Put the size into a jar, can, or bucket, pour on just a little cold water to soften it, and immediately precipitate the necessary quantity of boiling water into the vessel. Unless the boiling water is poured on directly the size is mixed with the cold water, the size will quickly set and will be useless. That is the main point to watch when making it. It should be applied warm to the wood, and care should be taken to see that too much is not put on, otherwise it would probably peel off in the course of time, taking the aftercoats with it. Carved work, mouldings, or very intricate parts, should be sized with a smaller brush than is used on broad, plain parts, and carefully wiped out to prevent the size collecting in quirks or recesses.

Spirit Varnish.—This will completely seal the pores of the finer woods, but is not recommended for general work, as stains do not adhere to it well.

Japanner's Gold Size and Turpentine.—These, when

Woods for Staining

used in equal quantities, prove excellent for soft or sappy wood.

Oil Varnish is especially good for oil stains, but it should be a hard varnish and thinned down a little with turpentine.

Should it be desired to lessen the number of finishing coats, the above could be used in exactly the same manner, as they are employed simply to stop the absorption of the wood. It should be noted, however, that they must not be used for chemical stains. As the best results are invariably obtained by allowing the stain to soak well into the pores of the wood, it follows that the foregoing should not be employed except under the circumstances indicated.

Fillers.—The question of " Fillers " comes next, but as we purpose dealing with them in the section on French Polishing very little will be said about them at this juncture. These are usually employed on the coarse, open-grained woods, as oak, ash, etc., being used to fill up the pores of the wood and thus present a nice level surface suitable for a high-class finish. The operation of filling may be performed on the bare wood or after the application of the stain, and consists in rubbing the material well into the pores either with a piece of rag or a short stiff brush. When it has set—which does not take more than half an hour or an hour—the work must be vigorously rubbed across the grain of the wood, thereby rubbing a portion of the surplus filler into some of the pores which may have been missed in the first application.

Coloured Fillers.—Some very striking effects are obtainable by means of coloured fillers. A transparent silex filler may be mixed with a dry pigment to make a coloured filler. This, when rubbed into the wood, causes the pores, or open part of the grain, to appear in colour, while the hard part of the grain retains its natural appearance. This treatment may be modified by first treating the wood with a stain, and, when dry, applying a coloured

Staining and Polishing

filler in the usual manner. For instance, the wood may be dyed a dark green, and a white filler used; then the grain will show up white on a dark green background. This method affords opportunity for the display of taste in colour effects. By finishing up pieces of spare board in various colours, the designer can in.this way get a clear idea of how it is going to look.

Puttying.—This is sometimes done before staining, and sometimes after. If the wood has to be left simply stained without any further finish, then the puttying must take place before the staining. In this case there is the risk of unskilled hands soiling the surface of the wood round about the joint or nail-hole to be filled by plastering the putty beyond the holes. If an oil putty is being used this will cause an oil mark on the surface, with the consequence that the subsequent stain will not penetrate as far into the wood as in other parts, and thus will turn out lighter in those places. To do the work successfully, only just sufficient putty to fill the hole should be taken up on the point of the putty knife, and put exactly in its place without touching the surface of the adjoining wood. For oil and spirit stains use ordinary oil putty, while for water stains and chemical stains use a putty made from two parts whiting and one part plaster-of-paris, mixed with suitably coloured polish.

Beaumontage or Hard Stopping is generally preferred to putty for the filling up of nail-holes or other small defects. Equal parts of beeswax and resin, with a little shellac added to it, are melted together in an iron ladle or glue-spoon; suitable dry colours, such as yellow ochre, brown umber or Venetian red, are then added, so as to give the mixture the desired shade. Beaumontage can be bought ready-made in three colours: satin-walnut, American walnut and mahogany. It is similar to a stick of sealing-wax, and it is run into the nail-hole or defect with the aid of a hot poker.

STAINING

APPLYING THE STAIN—A COLOUR CHART—COLOUR SCHEMES AND OPERATIONS—IMPREGNATED WOOD—EBONISING—STAINING WICKERWORK—DYEING WOODS

BRUSHWORK.—Before applying the stains to the work it is always best to experiment first on a spare piece of wood, and so avoid the danger of spoiling the original work. It must not be overlooked that to apply stains properly needs speed and good brushwork. This is particularly the case when using quick-drying stains, such as spirit or varnish stains. Water stains also require to be applied in a smart manner. Oil stains, being of a slow-drying nature, are the easiest to apply. The temperature of the room must also be taken into consideration, because if it is over-heated the stain will dry very quickly, and if not handled in an expert manner will look patchy and show all the laps or joinings. Hence good brushwork involves method in working.

The work in hand must be so arranged that not more than one edge needs to be kept " alive." By " keeping the edge alive " is meant the application of the second brushful of colour before the first has had time to set. Suppose we have to stain a two-panelled door with moulding and stiles. It is a common error to commence with the mouldings, and then apply a brushful to the middle of the panels, consequently having to work both ways from the centre of the panels to the sides, thus causing two edges to have to be kept alive, and when they come to the stiles overlapping at every joint. The result is that the door, when finished, presents a patchy and soiled appearance.

The correct way is to run a small brushful along the right-hand side of the panel close to the moulding, and then to take a large brushful and apply it close to the edge of the last application, and so on until the other side is reached, taking the precaution to finish off each brushful as soon as it is laid on. This finishing off simply consists in lightly

Staining and Polishing

drawing the brush across the stain, afterwards lightly brushing over with an up-and-down stroke. Great care must be taken in finishing the tops and bottoms of panels, as such places are liable to turn out lighter than the rest, owing to the brush partly drawing the stain away when finishing off. To prevent this, the brush should be lightly

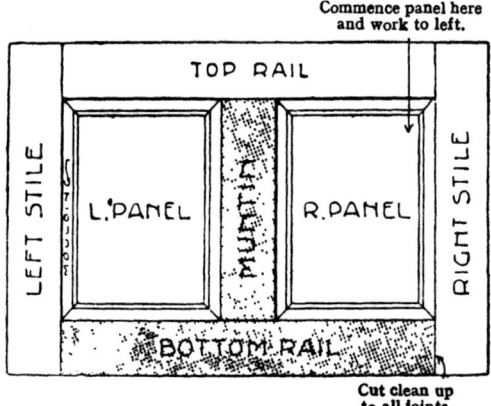

Fig. 1.—Diagram Illustrating the Method of Working the Various Parts.

swept upwards towards the moulding and downwards towards the bottom, taking care in doing so not to make a brush mark where the brush first strikes the panel. In regard to this last defect it should be borne in mind that it is more liable to occur on the top of a polished or varnished surface, or any non-absorbent surface, and when a slow-setting stain is employed.

When both panels are coated, take the muntin, top rail, bottom rail, and outside stiles in the order mentioned. Finally, cut in the mouldings very neatly with a fitch (Fig. 4). The rails and stiles have to be executed very carefully. The brush must not trespass on to the stiles

Staining

when doing the rails or on to the latter when doing the muntin or centre stile, as such touches invariably set before the parts can be stained completely. The best way to do this safely is to run a small tool or fitch along the joinings and then fill in the rest of that particular portion. When laps do occur, however, whether on panels, stiles, or else-

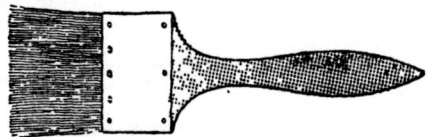

Fig. 2.—Large Flat Brush for Panels.

where, their appearance may be improved by scraping the brush dry, and then rubbing the defective parts with the side, or by wiping with a rag. Fig. 1 shows the door with the names for all the different parts and illustrates the manner of staining it.

Fig. 3.—Flat Tool.

In cases where heavy staining has to be resorted to, such as in rendering the appearance of mahogany to American whitewood, it is preferable to apply two or more coats of a weak stain, rather than build up the colour in one operation, a process which is liable to leave the surface of the wood with a " patchy " appearance. Further, in cases where it is not necessary that the grain of the wood should show up with particular distinction—a comparatively rare occurrence in dealing with heavy stained work—it is often desirable that the direct staining of the wood be stopped before it has become quite dark enough, the finishing of the colouring being carried out—in the earlier stages

Staining and Polishing

of the polishing—by means of stained polish, which tones down the surface and does away with that glaring effect so commonly seen in the cheaper kinds of stained work. Of course, much depends upon the kind of wood being dealt with, and also upon the results desired, and it must naturally be left to the discretion of the worker as to what kind of staining shall be employed; but, at the same time it

FIG. 4.—FLAT HOG-HAIR FITCH.

should be borne in mind that the aim of the polisher should be to hide the fact that the work has been stained. Stains penetrate and show much darker on the end grain of all woods; therefore the stain should be slightly weakened for this purpose or two distinct shades will show up on the finished work.

Brushes.—The best brushes for the purpose are flat, thin-toed ones. Fig. 2 represents the kind of brush indicated for larger work, and Fig. 3 a tool of the same pattern. Fig. 4 shows a flat fitch such as is recommended for mouldings.

Good quality brushes should not be used in applying chemical stains, as soda, lime, potash and most of the substances employed in this class of staining will destroy the bristles. If broad surfaces are to be stained a sponge should be used, though for mouldings, tracery work, or any kind of intricate detail work, the brush is best—in fact, indispensable.

Knotting.—A clear shellac polish, termed in the trade "knotting," may be utilised to advantage in staining. It is easily prepared by placing eight or nine ounces of orange or white lac in an earthenware vessel with one pint of methylated spirits, and agitating the same at intervals

Staining

until completely dissolved. It is then placed in a warm atmosphere, securely corked, and allowed to repose a few days, when it is ready for use. If coloured with bismarck brown it forms a good mahogany stain, which might be termed a varnish stain. A little vandyke brown will produce oak and walnut stains, less vandyke being used for the oak stain than for the walnut. By the addition of

FIG. 5.—STIPPLER.

various coloured aniline spirit dyes, almost any shade of varnish stain may be prepared. It becomes a " varnish " stain because of the presence of the gum or lac in the knotting ; without this it would simply be a spirit stain.

Spirit stains evaporate very quickly, and in consequence should not be used on large plain surfaces until a fair amount of dexterity with the brush has been acquired. They are suitable for picture frames, small objects of furniture, knick-knacks, and for fretwork ; but the method of working already outlined must be closely followed, otherwise disastrous results will attend the operation.

Stippling.—Oil stains are invariably of a slow-drying nature, and thus are more adapted to the use of beginners than the quick-setting stains. Great care must be taken

Staining and Polishing

with these to prevent "running," which is caused by the stain being applied too liberally, or not sufficiently brushed out. If the surface operated upon be new wood, then the oil stain will be absorbed before running takes place; but if the surface be a non-porous one, then the danger is much greater and it will be the best plan to stipple the stain immediately it is applied. This is effected by dabbing the stain evenly all over with a large dry brush, the ends of the bristles being firm, square, and even. Fig. 5 shows a proper stippler, but the reader need not go to the expense of purchasing a brush of this type, as a simpler and cheaper one will suffice provided it has the characteristics named.

A COLOUR CHART.

It must not be expected that satisfaction in staining can be obtained by careless and slipshod methods of working. To be able to execute any kind of staining, and to do it well, the worker must needs practise, and practise intelligently. Besides skill, which comes with intelligent practice, a certain amount of art enters into the work. This is evidenced by the choice of colours and their arrangement over the work in hand. A plan well worth adopting is to obtain a good selection of stains, dyes and colours, also a varied selection of natural woods, and then work out a colour chart. Although any wood may be used, the white woods are the best for ordinary staining, and canary, holly, and sycamore will perhaps suffice. A good chemist will stock most of the chemicals and dyes required and will also give any little information respecting the nature of such substances as the novice may desire. The cost is little, most of the chemicals required ranging from $1\frac{1}{2}d$. up to about $3d.$ per ounce. The aniline dyes are the most attractive, a vast range of colours being provided in this line, most of which cost (in normal times) not more than $6d.$ per ounce. The specially manufactured dyes called diamond and dolly dyes are sold in packets, and are more

Staining

expensive than those purchased by weight. It must be remembered that they are very powerful stains, and ¼ oz. of each will suffice for a beginning. They are in powder form, some being soluble in water, others in spirit, whilst some of them are soluble in both. Vinegar must be mixed with the anilines in water, as a mordant to fasten the colour. Always label the vessels in which you keep the various colours and dyes.

O	R.O.	R	R.P.	P	B.P.	B	B.G.	G	Y.G.	Y	Y.O.	O

FIG. 6.—COLOUR CHART.

R = Red.   B = Blue.   Y = Yellow (Primaries).
O = Orange.   P = Purple.   G = Green (Secondaries).
RO = Reddish Orange.   RP = Reddish Purple.
BP = Bluish Purple.   BG = Bluish Green.
YG = Yellowish Green.   YO = Yellowish Orange.

Mark the Wood into Squares, and apportion a square on the top row for each of the pure colours, to be equidistant from each other, and allowing a number of squares in between. Now commence by applying the pure stains in their allotted squares as strong as possible; then dilute them just a little with water, or spirit, or whatever the medium may be, and apply in the next square below, and so on, diluting gradually until the squares at the bottom present but a faint resemblance to the colours in the top squares.

Having got the full range of tones to be derived by dilution, next proceed to intermix the various colours. For instance, add a little yellow of the top row to the blue,

Staining and Polishing

and place it in the next square to the latter, in the same row. Keep adding a little more yellow until, midway between the two colours mentioned, green is obtained, and continue adding the yellow until it finally merges into that colour when you arrive at the next square to it. Proceed in the same way with all the others. The diagram on page 21 (Fig. 6) may help to make the matter clear. Only the three primary colours, red, yellow and blue, are given in the illustration, but the chart may be extended as desired. By this means the eye becomes familiar with the different colours, their tones and shades, and the worker also learns what colours he can obtain from the different dyes, etc. The reader with an instinct for art will find this subject intensely interesting, and we hope to increase this interest by treating of certain pleasing effects which can be obtained by stains, with the treatment of carved work and relief materials, and also by explaining the manner of dyeing woods.

COLOUR SCHEMES AND OPERATIONS.

We will now give very briefly a few suggestions of an interesting nature for staining. Woods that have a clearly marked and very definite grain, such as red or pitch pine, yield excellent results if they are given a full coat of stain, afterwards, while flowing wet, wiped off with rags. When the wiping is done with discrimination, the figure of the wood is brought out to the fullest extent and in sharp contrast. It will readily be seen that plain, even-grained woods are not so suitable for this purpose as the ones already mentioned. Oil stains are the best to use, as they are slow-drying; and as there are no risks of laps or brush marks by this method it is suitable for large surfaces. The best results are obtained when the stain is of a colour radically different from the wood, greens or blues being better than yellows.

Staining

STAINING RELIEF MATERIAL.

Wiping Out.—There is also to be considered the treatment of relief materials by wiping out. For those who cannot do wood-carving, a very good substitute is to procure some of the heavy relief material used by paper-hangers, such as anaglypta, lincrusta-walton, or lignomur. Various designs can be obtained and can be made to fit almost any given space. They can be fixed to wood with good strong flour paste. The material must, however, be prepared by first sizing, and then brought up with oil colour. A light buff ground is, perhaps, the most suitable to stain on, and the stain may be either in water or oil. The heights of the relief should be wiped pretty clean, and round the edges of the heights, or relief, the cloth should be dabbed or passed lightly over, to take away the harsh lines which might be made with the first wiping. For an oil stain ordinary soft cotton rag should be used to wipe off with, and for a water stain a damp chamois or wash-leather takes the place of the cotton rag.

To do the wiping, the cloth is rolled round the thumb, the left hand keeping the cloth tight. The particular portion of the cloth round the end of the thumb must be constantly changed, to keep the part of the cloth which is being used clean, otherwise the effect will be smudgy. In the case of operating on a typical piece of, say, lincrusta-walton, a dark green water stain may be used upon a pale yellow ground, and the wiping out then done with a chamois cloth.

Rich and brilliant effects can be got in this manner by using a dark green stain over a very pale one, or a bright red stain over a green one, etc. A little familiarity with the colour scale will suggest other combinations. This staining or glazing upon painted surfaces is usually termed "scumbling," but the process may well be included here, although the grain of the wood (when woods are used) is hidden. It is not, of course, intended that this class

Staining and Polishing

of work should be used upon beautifully-grained or mottled woods, but upon the coarser and unimportant varieties.

For Carved Work, the treatment advised for the relief paper designs applies equally well, but it is very rarely that this class of work is painted. In fact, it is not often that staining is employed, as oak, walnut, pear, plum and mahogany are usually retained in their natural colour and merely polished, the most popular method being wax-polishing. Where, however, staining is to take place, the surface must be made very smooth to prevent the wood swelling with the stain. For this purpose, rub well with a wad of very thin, soft shavings, firmly pressing with the hand until a faint lustre appears.

An antique shade on oak carvings may be produced by staining with umber which has been boiled in water with a little potash. Wood stained in this manner is not polished, but is usually varnished. Very fine effects can be obtained on carvings by wiping the high or prominent portions, and gradually blending down to the background.

Overglazing.—On fretwork and small furniture some beautiful effects can be got by applying one stain over another of a different colour. For instance, an article may be stained a bright green, and then given an overglaze of black or blue. Black or deep blue can be used to advantage over almost any bright colour, and gives a richness and mellowness of tone not to be obtained in any other way. Pitch pine, with suitable blue stains, will give really wonderful effects; whilst, if treated with a fine Spanish mahogany stain, it gives all the richness of Cuba mahogany. Again, apply a green stain on a good sample of yellow pine, and finish with a dull polish or varnish. This gives a peculiar metallic lustre, especially under artificial light. Many more such examples could be given, but sufficient has been said to suggest to the reader the possibilities that lie in the judicious use of stains.

Staining

Matching.—Sometimes a piece of wood is darker in some parts than in others, due to the sap edge being included. Whatever the cause, if it be desired to bring the wood as nearly as possible to one uniform colour, then one of the following methods must be adopted—either to bleach the darker parts, or to darken the lighter portions.

To Bleach a dark patch, make a fairly strong solution of oxalic acid (about 2 ozs. to a pint of hot water), and wash this carefully over the parts that have to be lightened. Two or three applications may be necessary, but this depends upon the nature of the stain in the wood, or upon the strength of the solution. It is afterwards necessary to coat the parts with common vinegar to kill the acid, or disastrous results may follow. This solution is also useful for cleaning dirt from corners, quirks and similar places.

Darkening.—The darkeners generally used are lime, ammonia, logwood, dyed oil, and various chemicals, such as nitric acid, nitrate of silver, sulphate of iron, etc. But the necessary darkening may generally be obtained by giving extra coats of stain over those parts, or a small quantity of colouring matter may be added to the polish. There is also the deepening of the natural colour of the wood with red oil and other colouring matter, according to the colour of the wood to be deepened; but these considerations really come under the head of French polishing, and we shall reserve further information until we arrive at the stage when these items must be more fully dealt with.

Fuming.—The darkening process, known as fuming or fumigating, is described on page 125, in a chapter dealing with the treatment of oak.

IMPREGNATED WOOD.

On the Continent much more rapid strides have been made with regard to wood impregnation. Freshly cut logs of timber have their watery and floating wood-sap removed

Staining and Polishing

by hydraulic pressure. In this manner the sap of the wood, which consists of easily decomposable albumen and saccharine, is removed and the food for insects destroyed. For the preservation of the wood, especially in tropical climates, this destruction of the food for insects (white ants, etc.) is invaluable.

The wood so treated is much more impervious to the effects of changes in weather or temperature, as the fibres are freed from the decompositions of the sap, and they become exceedingly hard and firm, so that contraction or cracking of the wood is reduced to a minimum. Not only can the wood be impregnated with any desired colour, which nothing can alter, being even acid-resisting, but its durability is greatly increased by the impregnation of rot-destroying substances. The colouring material does not merely adhere to the surface of the wood, as in the case of wood stains; it becomes indissolubly absorbed in the wood tissues. From a hygienic point of view, too, wood treated by this process is highly desirable for such purposes as flooring, panelled walls, ceilings and parquetry, on account of its want of attraction to all insect life. The process has been patented, and many of the leading furniture firms show furniture such as harewood, which is of a silvery grey colour. Alderwood, hornbeam, sycamore, and birchroot are impregnated with a full range of art colours. (See also page 29 for Dyeing Woods.)

EBONISING.

As natural ebony is so very expensive it is usually imitated by means of stains, an advantage being that the black, or nearly black, of the real wood is so easily imitated that it is difficult to distinguish between the genuine and the counterfeit article. Besides being costly the real wood is also hard to cut, and a rather softer wood, artificially stained, is sometimes substituted on that account. Although the real wood is not always black, it is represented by a black-stained wood, and as it is so popular in fancy furni-

Staining

ture, in overlays and in silhouette portraits and designs, we will give the ingredients and the mixing of a suitable stain.

An aniline black dye may be used, or several coats of Indian ink, or gas-black, or what is known as the French black stain; but the following cannot fail to satisfy, though it may appear to be a somewhat complicated mixture: Boil ½ lb. of logwood in 3 quarts of water until it has boiled down to 2 quarts, when a handful of walnut peeling must be added. Let this mixture boil for a further three hours. During the boiling add 1 pint of boiling-hot vinegar.

When this solution has boiled down to about half its original bulk it will be in a fit condition for use. Give the work to be stained a good flowing coat of the hot mixture, but be careful not to let it run all over the edges, etc. Before this has properly dried apply another coat of the same liquid, and do the same a third time. The stain gets a firmer grip upon the wood by applying one coat before the preceding one is dry. When the third coat is nearly dry commence to lay on a solution made by dissolving ½ oz. green copperas in 1 pint of hot water. This second solution might be prepared whilst the first solution is boiling. It is not absolutely necessary that two coats of this second mixture should be applied, though a second coat will ensure a denser black. The reader will find other recipes for ebonising in the Appendix.

Apple, pear, sycamore, cherry and holly are the best woods for ebonising, the closeness of the grain being more suitable for this purpose than soft open-grained woods. It is possible to dye oak to resemble ebony by soaking it for forty-eight hours in a hot solution of alum, and then painting it with a decoction of one part campeachy wood in 11 pints of water. This should be boiled down to one-half its volume, and 10 to 15 drops of neutral indigo tincture added for every quart of the mixture. After the application of this solution rub well with a saturated solution of verdigris in vinegar, and repeat the operation until the desired

Staining and Polishing

tint is obtained. Ebony is best finished dull, either wax-polished, or with bright polish rubbed down until an egg-shell gloss is obtained.

Another Method is to use French black stain. When dry, brush the work well with a dry stiff brush, oil with linseed oil, and give a rubber of white polish, which has been stained black by mixing a small quantity of gas-black in it. Fill in with tallow and plaster filler, which has also been stained with gas-black, and polish with white polish, which should be stained by grinding a little prussian blue and a little gas-black together very finely with a palette knife. This will produce a good black, and the work may be finished bright or dull.

If a dull finish is desired, the work should be left free from oil, dulled down with ground pumice stone or crocus powder, and rubbed over lightly with a piece of wadding, rubbing always in the direction of the grain. If the work is afterwards brushed over with a brush (an ordinary boot-polishing brush will answer) a very dull surface may be obtained. Coarse-grain oak may be made black and the grain left open by staining with French black stain. When dry, oil with linseed oil, and give a few rubbers of black polish.

STAINING WICKER-WORK.

Osiers or wicker goods are generally coloured with water stains. The work is first mordanted as follows: Take ¼ lb. best white unscented soap and dissolve it in 6 pints of boiling water, soak the wicker-ware in this solution and let it dry. The stain should be made by dissolving aniline dye of the required colour in water of about 90° Fahr. Stir the stain well and steep the wicker-work until the colour is deep enough. As the stain will become exhausted, it should be strengthened from time to time by the addition of freshly made dye solution. The aniline dyes used for the purpose must of course be those soluble in water. The following formulæ give the quantities to be used:—

Staining

Blue.—Dissolve 3 ozs. bengal blue in 3½ pints of boiling water, stir and filter the fluid through fine cambric after twelve minutes.

Green.—Dissolve 3 ozs. methyl green and ½ oz. bleu de lumière in ½ gallon of hot water.

Red.—Dissolve 3 ozs. of coral red in 5 pints of lukewarm water.

Violet.—Dissolve 3 ozs. of methyl violet in ½ gallon of lukewarm water.

Golden Yellow.—Dissolve 3 ozs. of naphthaline yellow in ½ gallon of water.

Brown.—Dissolve 3 ozs. bismarck brown in ½ gallon of water.

The quantities stated make a very heavy stain and they may be diluted with water to the required tint. Spirit varnish in the usual way.

DYEING WOODS.

Before proceeding to the treatment of various woods, a word may be said on the process of dyeing woods or veneers. This differs from staining, inasmuch as the wood when dyed is coloured right through, while only the surface, or very little more, is coloured by staining. In selecting wood for dyeing, for any colour except black, white wood should be used, such as sycamore, holly, beech, lime, etc. The tint is neutralised if a coloured wood be used. Beech, cherry, pear, or soft mahogany may be used for black, all these woods taking the stain well.

The qualities of dye-stuffs are considerably enhanced by the addition of a mordant to modify and fasten the shades they impart. Mordants are chemical preparations, and the chief are obtained from iron, tin, copper, aluminium, potash, soda, etc. ; whilst the colouring substances embrace

Staining and Polishing

vegetable roots and barks and berries, with acids and anilines. For dyeing, soak the veneer in water about a day ; then take it out and allow it to drain off for a few hours before placing it in the dye-bath. This opens the pores of the wood and thereby allows the dye to soak well in. But a more drastic and effective method is to boil the wood in a solution composed of $\frac{1}{2}$ lb. caustic soda to every 5 pints of water, the wood to be boiled in the solution for half an hour, and then allowed to remain in to soak for another twenty-four hours or so. Then take it out and wipe it well with clean shavings to remove the alkali, when it will be found to have become as soft as leather and equally plastic. Place it between boards, put some weights on to prevent warping, and let it remain until dry. This treatment cleans the pores from all gummy or resinous matter, so that it will absorb the dye-stuff like a sponge. The wood is then ready for the dye-bath. In the Appendix will be found various recipes for stains and dyes.

STAINING

Treatment of Various Woods

ALTHOUGH stains may be looked upon as a means of making woodwork appear to be that which it is not, they form a very necessary part of the polisher's kit, and are quite indispensable, not only for rendering to common woods the appearance of a superior quality, but for equalising the colours of hardwoods.

American Whitewood.—Dealing first with the colouring of inferior woods to represent the more expensive kinds, we find that American whitewood forms about the best groundwork for imitating mahogany, walnut and rosewood. It is occasionally useful also for ebonising, although the best ebonised furniture, etc., is made of mahogany and stained. American whitewood, sometimes called canary wood, canary pine, magnolia, canoe wood, saddle tree (on account of its peculiar leaf) and poplar, is one of the most suitable woods for stained work. A soft variety, it is not so soft as ordinary white or yellow pine. It is easily worked, and it is cheap, and when stained to represent mahogany or walnut the grain is a very good imitation of either.

Pine.—If pine of the best class can be obtained, nothing better can be had so far as working is concerned ; but, unfortunately, the best pine is difficult to obtain, and is also costly ; cheap pine is worse than nothing. Another disadvantage is the softness of the wood, and as all the woods which have to be represented by staining are hard, more or less, the liability to damage from this cause at once discloses the fact that the work is only an imitation.

Kauri Pine is sometimes recommended for staining ; but it works up very rough, though easy to get up well. Its great defect is the liability to curl and twist, which

Staining and Polishing

prevents its use for furniture to any great extent, and it is not to be compared to American whitewood, either for ease in working, price, or stability.

Pitch Pine may be polished in its natural colour, and very soon tones to a rich shade. It may be filled in with a little yellow ochre, polished with button polish, and finished bright. It is also stained green for school furniture, etc. Almost every other description of pine will stain and polish well by following the directions given for satin walnut; but if required in its natural colour, it may be filled with a mixture of clean tallow and plaster-of-paris and polished with white polish. Any variety of pine may be stained and varnished with very good results, and will wear well, if carefully stained. When dry give a coat of warm tub size, and varnish with hard oak coburg or copal varnish; if a high gloss is required, two coats may be given.

To darken Pine before varnishing, first stain with equal quantities of japan gold size and turpentine, to which has been added the necessary colouring material, such as burnt or raw umber, burnt sienna or black, and afterwards finish with two or three coats of the best extra hard church oak varnish.

Birch is usually finished in its natural colour when not stained to imitate other woods. It should be filled in with tallow and plaster-of-paris filler. Great care must be taken that the grain is well filled, for if any parts are missed these will always show darker and the work will have a patchy appearance. It may be polished with white polish or with button polish. As the grain of birch has a tendency to rise, it will be necessary in some cases to paper down with flour glass-paper a second time. Birch may be stained to imitate mahogany, when its darker grain becomes more pronounced. If this should be required, stain with bismarck brown and powdered brown water stain; when dry, oil with linseed oil and give a coat of button polish. Fill in

Staining

with plaster and tallow filler tinted with red lake, and polish with button polish tinted with a little bismarck brown. Birch may also be stained to walnut by using brown powdered water stain, and when dry with plaster and tallow filler tinted with powdered vandyke brown, and polished with button polish.

Birch is a popular wood for furniture and interior finish. Heavy and strong, its colour is a light reddish-brown, and it has a fine compact grain. Silver grey is a very attractive finish for birch. (See note on silver oak stain on page 130.) As a foundation for white enamel effect it is unsurpassed. Its light colour and delicate grain make it suitable for this purpose.

Satin Walnut may be polished in its natural colour, or stained and polished to almost any shade. This wood is equally valuable for staining to imitate mahogany, oak, walnut, or rosewood. If it is required to be finished in its natural colour, it must be filled in with Russian tallow, stained with yellow ochre, and polished with button polish and finished bright. To imitate mahogany, prepare a stain by mixing bismarck brown and powdered brown stain with water to the tint required, and apply with a hog's-hair brush. When dry, oil with linseed oil and give a coat of button polish; fill in with tallow stained with red lake, and polish with button polish tinted with bismarck brown.

A good rosewood stain can be made by mixing bismarck brown and a little dry ground drop black with water. Lay off with a stiff brush; by this means the light and dark veins are produced. When dry, oil and give a coat of button polish, fill in with tallow stained with a little dry ground drop black and red lake, and polish with button polish tinted with a little bismarck brown.

For oak, mix powdered brown water stain with water, and lay off carefully so that an even colour is produced. When dry, oil with linseed oil and give a coat of button polish; or fill in with tallow stained with dry brown umber, and polish with button polish.

Staining and Polishing

Walnut stain is made by adding a little dry ground drop black to powdered brown water stain. When dry, fill in with tallow tinted with vandyke brown, and polish with button polish.

Satin walnut may also be stained green, in which case green powdered water stain will be found the best. If a dark shade of green is required, add a little powdered brown stain, and when dry fill in with tallow tinted with a little powdered middle brunswick green, and polish with white polish, or it may be wax-polished.

Sycamore can be dyed grey by the use of blue copperas. The wood must be well covered by the boiling dye, or results will not be satisfactory. The bath must be heated by some means, as the dye must be kept on the boil for some considerable time. First of all, boil sufficient water in the bath, then add some pearlash, about 2 or 3 ozs. to the gallon. Place the wood into this, and allow to boil for an hour, then take out and place into the boiling dye. If only one bath is being used, the pearlash solution must be quickly run off and the dye got ready as soon as possible. To make this, run sufficient water into the bath, and while this is heating add the copperas, which should be broken up as small as possible to help it to dissolve the quicker. Copperas is very cheap, and may be purchased from any druggist. There are three kinds (white, blue and green). The dye must not be too strong, but should rather be on the weak side, say, about $\frac{1}{2}$ lb. to the gallon. When it has got to the boil add common vinegar in the proportion of about 1 quart to the gallon of water. Next place the wood in, and leave to boil for from one to two hours, according to the strength of the dye; then turn the heat off and leave all alone for a few hours. The wood must be taken out and well dried.

Baywood.—On baywood (sometimes called bay mahogany) oil has little darkening effect, and the colour will therefore have to be brought up by the application of a

Staining

weak mahogany stain, this being followed, if practicable, by stained polish. Baywood is a common substitute for both Spanish and Honduras mahogany, and, although baywood has the mahogany grain, it lacks prominence of figuring and also depth of colour, and has therefore to be darkened down previous to or in course of polishing in order that the finished work may be rich in tone.

Spanish and Cuban Mahogany darken considerably upon the application of oil to their surface, but not sufficiently so as to render the wood dark enough for " dark mahogany " or Chippendale effects, which latter necessitate a further colouring down of the material. One of the most useful darkening agents known to polishers is that made by dissolving bichromate of potash (called " chroma " in the trade) in water. A stock solution of chroma should always be kept at hand, and this should be of full strength —*i.e.*, the crystals of bichromate should be allowed to soak until the water will not take up any more of the chemical, and when required for use the solution can, if necessary, be diluted.

The action of bichromate of potash on wood is not a direct one, as when it is applied to the surface it merely stains it yellow, and unless it is allowed to come into contact with daylight it remains this colour. Gaslight has comparatively little effect in darkening the chroma, and therefore operations in this direction should be carried out in daylight, but not in direct sunlight. When the tone of the wood is found to be that which is desired, the work should be wiped over with raw linseed oil, which stops further darkening.

In inlaid work, especially, is the use of chroma found to be of benefit, as its action on the woods of which the inlays are generally made is not nearly so fast as on darker woods, and consequently the inlays show up to good advantage against their dark background. In toning down walnut, rosewood, etc., both plain and inlaid, chroma is also useful.

Staining and Polishing

Italian Walnut is often used as a substitute for rosewood, but of course it will be readily understood that burr and bird's-eye walnut are quite unsuited for the purpose. The straight-grained wood, with long black figuring, is the kind required, and this has to be coloured with mahogany water or spirit stain until the requisite colour is obtained, while, if a particularly dark effect is required, a weak solution of chroma can be first applied, leaving out the oiling of the wood until the whole of the staining has been done.

Rosewood is a rather expensive wood to use, even when veneering is resorted to, and a substitute for this wood is found in ordinary Italian walnut, which, although it lacks the requisite colour, has very frequently a similarity of figure and grain. Of course staining has to be resorted to in order to get the rosewood colour.

In polishing rosewood great care must be taken that only as little oil as possible is used, or the work will commence sweating shortly after it is finished. This applies more or less to all woods that have to be oiled first, but especially to rosewood. Consequently, after oiling, rub as dry as possible before laying on the polish, then fill in carefully, as the grain is very coarse, and if any part is missed in filling a very uneven surface will be the result. Any light parts may be shaded by mixing a little gas-black with red polish, to match as near as possible. Unless this is done, some parts will always look poor; but by using a little care the matching can be rendered practically imperceptible.

Walnut.—American, English, and Italian walnut should be treated as follows: All parts must be carefully oiled, and allowed to stand for some time; this will bring up the colour of the wood much better. Any light parts should then be stained by mixing powdered walnut water stain made to the required strength; or if only shading is necessary, English and Italian may be treated by mixing finely-

Staining

ground dry vandyke brown with yellow polish, and applying it with a camel-hair brush, following the direction of the grain of the wood as much as possible. If, as is often the case with burr or figured walnut, a very plain piece is jointed on to a figured piece, vein to match with a small camel-hair pencil. American walnut may be matched by mixing purple brown and vandyke brown and yellow polish to the shade required; apply with a camel-hair brush and then polish with yellow polish, following the instructions given for polishing mahogany.

Oak.—The treatment of oak—including fumigating—is dealt with in a separate chapter (see page 125).

In Finishing Off work which has to be stained, great care should be taken to get a good face, and on no account to rub the glass-paper across the grain, or the work will be spoiled. All nail holes should be stopped with glue and whitening mixed, or with hard stopping, and tinted to match the bare wood as nearly as possible (see reference to "Beaumontage" or hard stopping, on page 14).

The stain should, as a rule, be put on plentifully, so that every part is covered, taking especial care of all quirks and mouldings; and when nearly dry, rub over with a dry rag. This has the effect of levelling down the tint, as it were, and does away with all uneven parts. For varnished work it should then be sized with fairly strong size, and, lastly, varnished with good varnish. Do not be discouraged if the size forms a lather, as this will go off when dry.

STAINING FLOOR MARGINS.

A common method of staining floor margins is to use burnt umber (in oil), mixing with liquid driers, raw linseed oil, and turpentine. According to the quantity of thinners used, the stain will be suitable for imitating light walnut or even very dark walnut. Very often floors are done a solid colour, such as a dark brown or chocolate, in which

Staining and Polishing

case more umber must be added to the above, or else two coats given.

An oak stain may be made by mixing raw sienna (in oil) with driers, oil and turpentine, as before. A mahogany colour may be obtained by using Venetian red for a quiet tone, or mahogany lake for a brighter hue, both had in oil, and mixed with the same ingredients as given for the other stains above.

Of course, the staining may be done in water if desired, in which case the colours already mentioned should be had in water instead of oil. But oil stains are preferable for floors, being more durable than those in water, and do not raise the grain so much.

A cheap and rich mahogany stain in water may be made by using permanganate of potash. Rub the stain well into all cracks and joints, and after the stain is dry fill up any joints needed with putty stained to match. This applies to oil staining, the stain forming a key for the putty, and holding it well in place. The floor may be either oil or wax-polished, but the quickest way is to coat with oil varnish. Use best church oak varnish, as this will dry hard. The floor may afterwards be rubbed over with beeswax and turpentine or furniture paste from time to time. Sandpaper well before varnishing.

FRENCH POLISHING

SHELLAC—THE POLISHING WORKSHOP AND EQUIPMENT—
THE POLISHING RUBBER

ALTHOUGH French polishing is a trade by itself, it is only natural that every woodworker will wish to finish his own work without having recourse to a professional polisher. The difficulties in the way are not great for anyone who is prepared to exercise a fair amount of care and patience in the work, and when properly done there is no better surface to be obtained. And firstly, a word must be said on the essential medium in French polishing—shellac.

SHELLAC.

Shellac is made from lac, or gum lac, a resinous substance which comes from the branches of several trees; the most common is the *Fiscus religiosa* (the religious tree of the Hindus); the *Rhamnus jujuba*, and the *Croton lacciferum* (behar tree). These trees grow in Siam, Assam, Bengal and Malabar. An insect (the female insect of *Coccus lacca*) punctures the bark of these trees for the purpose of depositing her eggs; the resinous substance oozes from the tree and hardens on the twigs. The twigs are broken off by the natives and dried in the sun. When dried these are called stick lac. After the twigs have become thoroughly dry they are pounded so as to break the resinous substance from the twigs. This resinous substance, after being removed from the twigs, is known as seed lac. Seed lac is melted, collected, and cooled, and it is then known as lump lac.

The seed lac is put into bags made of cotton and hung over a slow fire; the resinous substance now melts, and the bag is twisted and the clean filtered substance is allowed to flow over planks generally made of fig wood, the timber

Staining and Polishing

of which is hard and smooth. The resinous substance cools on these planks, forming thin layers or scales, which are known to commerce as *shell-lac* or shellac.

White or Bleached Shellac is made from the brown shellac by passing chlorine (one of the most powerful bleaching agents) through it. The colouring matter is thus taken out, giving the familiar white shellac of commerce. Bleached shellac should be put into alcohol or methylated spirit as soon as it is dry. If exposed to the air for a few days it oxidises and becomes partially insoluble. Bleached shellac should therefore be kept under water, and transported by burying it in wet sawdust. To dry white shellac before making it into polish, the lac should be finely broken up and spread out upon a tray, which is placed before a slow fire. The broken lac should be frequently turned over on the tray until all moisture has disappeared.

WHAT FRENCH POLISHING IS.

French Polish is thus but a varnish, though of a different nature from the ordinary oil varnishes. The chief difference lies in the application. Ordinary varnishes are laid on with a brush, with as little friction as possible, whereas French polish is applied by means of rubbers worked over the surface of the wood with a light pressure, and the more rubbing the polish receives (up to a certain point) the better the results. Briefly, then, the great distinction is attributable to French polish being applied as scantily as possible by rubbers, and needing much friction and many applications, whilst varnish is applied as freely as possible with a brush, causing as little friction as possible and a high polish being obtained by only a few applications.

Skill is necessary to make a good polisher, as well as knowledge about the materials and their manipulation. The skill, of course, is only to be acquired with practice. Some people regard French polishing as a mystery, rather

French Polishing

than as an art to be acquired. On early attempts the refusal of the polish to come up satisfactorily under one's hands is indeed mysterious. French polishing looks such easy work that the baffled novice may be pardoned for thinking he has got hold of the wrong stuff, or that he has been misdirected; and though either circumstance may be the cause of failure, it is much more likely to be want of skill. Everything will here be done to remove difficulties and to indicate right methods of working. The rest will depend upon the polisher himself.

Care and Patience are, apart from skill, two essentials in the polisher's art. The work must on no account be unduly hurried, every detail having to receive its due share of attention. Practice is vital. Success can only come by continued application to the work, owing to the fact that the "touch" or amount of pressure put upon the rubber must in a large degree be acquired, and is not an operation which can be adequately conveyed by written or verbal description.

Quality.—It might be argued that there ought to be only one quality in French polishing—the best. In actual practice there are widely different qualities, the quality value depending upon the time expended in its execution, and in a lesser degree on the quality and kind of materials. Cheap work necessitates the application of a thick coating put on quickly, this being usually done with a brush, and the finishing carried out as soon as the brush coat is dry enough to work on without "picking up." In this way polishing can be started and finished the same day, but of course it cannot be compared with work which has been given numerous thin coats, each of which has received a proper amount of attention and been allowed sufficient time to dry before an attempt was made to put on the next.

Old Methods.—That all woodwork when left by the cabinet-maker or joiner presents an unfinished appearance is admitted by nearly everyone who has the least regard

Staining and Polishing

for appearances. In days gone by it was a rule in most houses to set apart one day of the week for polishing the household furniture, fitments, floors, etc., and it was with pardonable pride that our grandmothers used to show their visitors the polished tables and other articles. The recipes for making the polish were carefully preserved, and, although many differed as to the exact proportion of the ingredients used, it would be found on comparison that they were composed chiefly of beeswax and resin or yellow soap, liquefied with turpentine.

There is no doubt that the labour expended did not always give the result desired and, in many cases, deserved; consequently, when French polishing was introduced into England in the first half of the last century, it advanced rapidly in favour in place of the older methods, and by the year 1851, when the first International Exhibition was held, it had been generally adopted. The reason for this is not far to seek. The colour of the finished article was more uniform, the grain was seen to much better advantage, and the general effect, especially on inlaid work, improved. When the work was well executed, a vast amount of labour was saved, as with care the polish would last for a number of years.

THE POLISHING WORKSHOP.

The Polishing Room.—In French polishing certain requirements are necessary, and, if good work is to be turned out, will be found to be indispensable. The workshop must be well lighted, kept free from dust, and, as much as possible, kept at an even temperature. Good results cannot be obtained in a dark, dirty, damp, or cold workshop, and the work, if attempted under such conditions, will take a much longer time to execute, and then be unsatisfactory.

The polisher must have his polish mixed and ready for use, his rubbers made, and all necessary materials, tools,

French Polishing

and appliances in proper order and easy of access. The room must possess a decent window, and be so convenient as to allow of the place being heated in cold, damp weather to equal the ordinary summer temperature of 60° or 70°. Whether the room be heated by means of pipes or stove or fire does not very much matter, but something must be done to check the intrusion of the chilly and frosty air, or the results of the efforts at polishing will have been in vain.

Equipment.—It is also advisable to have a few canvas wrappers to work on, both for cleanliness and to prevent the polished object from getting scratched or otherwise damaged. Cotton ones, if free from dust, may be used to cover up with after the polisher has finished work for the day. This helps to keep the dust off the articles, some of which is always flying about in the air, even when we cannot see it.

A few bottles, both pints and gills, should be at hand for the different polishes, and also for spirits, raw linseed oil, red oil, etc. Some pots or jam-jars will be needed for holding ground pumice stone, and for straining polish to which has been added some of the colouring substances. For straining purposes fine muslin is best, and a quantity of this should be stored. Pots or canisters will also be required for holding plaster-of-paris, whiting, dry colours, beeswax, shellac, rottenstone, size, etc. For rubbing down, a quantity of fine glass-paper will be needed, in addition to some felt (an old felt hat will do) and a clean shoe brush for purposes of dulling. The latter will also be needed for wax polishing. Procure also a liberal quantity of cotton wadding, either white or brown (though preferably the former) and some good soft cotton-rag or calico, which must be perfectly clean and free from dust. These materials are to be used for making the rubbers. A soft camel-hair brush, termed a gilder's mop, will also be required in addition to a few small brushes known as "pencils." The former is for laying the polish on plain surfaces (when it

Staining and Polishing

is found necessary to use a brush), and the latter are for use on narrow moulds, quirks, or any part where the mop would be too large to use without incurring the danger of overlapping on to another portion of the work.

It will also be found advisable to have a small bag for holding fine pumice-stone powder, and which is called a pounce-bag. To make this, procure a piece of muslin or some clean rag of moderately open texture, and cut to about 6 ins. square. Lay it out on the bench or table and put a small handful of pumice powder in the centre. Gather up the corners together, give a slight twist, and then tie a length of string tightly round the neck of the bag. Do not fasten the pumice up tight, but let the bag proper be slack, so that when dabbed on to the work a quantity of the powder will be shaken through the rag. It is essential that the bag be kept perfectly clean, and not allowed to lie about on the bench, or it will pick up dirt. To prevent this it is advisable, when tying on the string, to leave a loop so that the bag may be hung up on a nail in a clean place. Fig. 15 (page 48) shows the kind of bag to be used.

THE POLISHING RUBBER.

A large employer of labour once remarked to the writer that he could tell if a man was a competent French polisher the moment he saw him wrap up his rubber. There is certainly much truth in this statement, because, should the rag covering not be neatly folded and twisted up, thus keeping the rubber free from creases, the surface of the work to which it is applied will, when finished, be "ropey," "stringy," and full of ridges.

Moulding the Rubber.—The wad or rubber proper (Fig. 7) is made by taking a piece of white sheet wadding about 4 ins. by 2¾ ins., and carefully removing the skin. Double it in half and squeeze it in the hand until it is moulded to a similar shape to that shown at Fig. 8. Next lay it on another piece of white wadding about 4 ins. by

French Polishing

3 ins., as at Fig. 8, and proceed to wrap it up in exactly the same manner as though the outer layer of wadding was a rag covering; but, instead of twisting up the ends when arriving at stage Fig. 11, simply fold them on top of the pad you have already formed and press all into a good shape. Rubbers, of course, will vary in size.

FIG. 7.—THE POLISHING RUBBER WRAPPED IN RAG; IT SHOULD BE PEAR-SHAPED AND NEATLY FORMED AS INDICATED.

FIG. 8.—THE RUBBER PLACED ON ITS RAG.

Wrapping the Rubber.—Place the rubber as at Fig. 8 on a piece of fine well washed rag about 6 ins. by 4 ins., taking care that the rag is free from lint and dust. Now turn

FIG. 9.—FIRST STAGE OF WRAPPING.

over the rag on to the cotton wad as at Fig. 9, and press it down close to the rubber at each side of the wad as

Staining and Polishing

indicated by the shading. Next take the part marked A, Fig. 9, and fold it over the rubber as shown at Fig. 10. The part marked B in Fig. 10 is now folded over A, and the result is seen at Fig. 11. The whole of the rag at the back

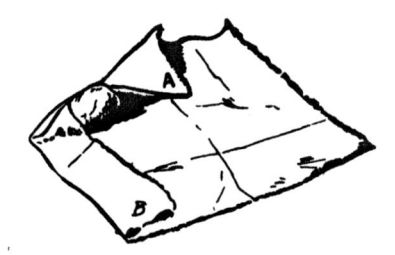

FIG. 10.—SECOND STAGE OF WRAPPING.

of the rubber is then twisted up, and the familiar polishing rubber as shown at Fig. 13 is the result. Fig. 12 shows the method of holding a rubber charged with polish, the single line indicating the circular path given to the rubber whilst in use.

For ordinary purposes two rubbers will be sufficient, one for fatting and bodying-up, and the other for spiriting-off.

FIG. 11.—THIRD STAGE OF WRAPPING.

Charging the Rubber with Polish.—To charge a rubber with polish *the rag covering should always be removed*, and the polish dropped on to the wadding. A good method

French Polishing

is to keep the polish in an ordinary medicine bottle and to cork the bottle with a sprinkler top cork as used in scent bottles. Failing this, cut a small groove at each side of the ordinary cork so as to allow a little of the liquid to exude

FIG. 12.—How to hold the Rubber.

FIG. 13.—Correct Shape of Rubber.

FIG. 14.—Wrong Form of Rubber.

from the bottle as is required. Only sufficient polish should be put upon the wad to moisten it, and to just appear through the rag when pressure is applied ; the polish may

Staining and Polishing

be evenly distributed throughout the rubber by pressing it with the ball of the thumb.

If, after the rubbers have been in use, they are left lying about and exposed to the air, they will become hard and

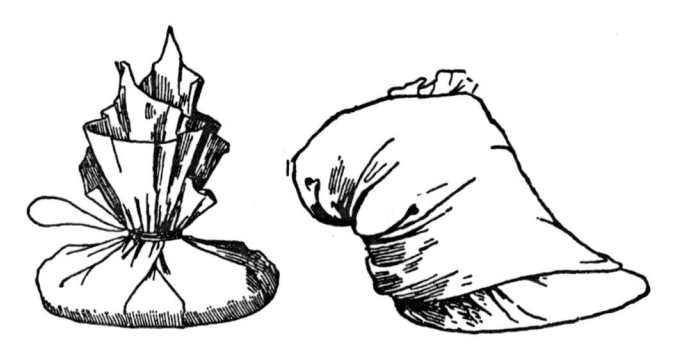

FIG. 15.—POUNCE BAG.   FIG. 16.—SIDE VIEW OF RUBBER.

unfit for further use. It is therefore necessary to keep them in an airtight tin, so that they may remain soft and can be used again at a moment's notice. When rubbers are not in use for a few days, a few drops of methylated spirit should be sprinkled inside the tin to keep them moist.

PREPARING FURNITURE FOR FRENCH POLISHING

PREPARING SURFACES—PREPARING NEW WOOD—WAX STOPPING—FILLERS AND FILLING

THE success of polishing very largely depends upon having a good sweep for the manipulation of the rubbers. Where corners have to be got into there is a momentary stoppage between putting the rubber in and taking it out, during which the polish is liable to pick up or adhere to the rubber, and it is therefore necessary to take the work to pieces as far as is practicable. In furniture of good quality and design the construction is so arranged as to admit of the parts being separated in order that repolishing can be properly done. In the fixing of the smaller parts of good furniture screws are used instead of the nails and glue found in cheap grade work.

All Brasswork, such as handles, hinges, etc., should be removed from work being polished, and mirrors and glass should be taken out. All doors, panels, shelves, and parts which can be removed without injury to the article are more easily worked up on the bench, and therefore should be separated from the carcase work. Dressing tables fitted with trinket drawers, etc., should have the framings which hold the drawers removed from the top board in order to provide a flat run on the top, which, if screwed up from underneath, should be removed.

In cases where overlay carvings are used, these will have to be taken off carefully to avoid splitting them; a wide chisel, with a piece of thin wood put underneath the blade to act as a fulcrum and prevent the surface being damaged, will be found the best means of raising overlay ornaments. In cases where it is possible to remove mouldings and beadings without fear of injury this should

Staining and Polishing

be done, as it is then far easier to carry out the polishing. In the very best classes of new work the moulds and beads are cut and fitted, but left unfixed, so that the polishers can almost finish them before they are in position.

Pianos are always considered to be the most difficult of all furniture to polish, owing to the fact that the finish on these instruments has always to be of the finest. In piano work it is essential that all removable obstructions should be separated from the main part. The top lid, if in one piece, should be taken off and the hinges removed, or if it is what is termed a halved lid the front piece should be removed and the hinge taken off. The top door has to be taken from the carcase and divested of sconces, panels and mouldings, unless the latter are at the extreme ends and not fixed by screws, when no attempt should be made to remove them. The fall which covers the keys, together with its continuation to the back, must come out and the two pieces separated by undoing the hinge. The desk must also be unscrewed from its support and the bottom door underneath the keys should receive a treatment similar to that bestowed upon the top door. This practically completes the taking to pieces of a piano, unless it is preferred that the keys be removed. This will necessitate taking the action out first—which should not be attempted unless the worker understands the interior mechanism of pianos. Any polish which may get on the edges of the keys can be easily removed by the application of a little methylated spirit.

Upholstered Furniture should be polished before the covering is put on, as it is far more convenient to handle, and the risk of damaging the cover is thus done away with. If, however, it is necessary to carry out the polishing while the coverings are on, remove the gimp or banding, and run pieces of paper between the cover and the back legs, so that the rubber can be worked well down to the cover. Pin-cushion work, which is finished off with brass nails,

Preparing Furniture for French Polishing

can have the polish rubbed off the nails with methylated spirit applied with a piece of rag and a stick of wood as a support. Cane-seat chairs should, where possible, have the caning (or recaning) done just before the polishing is finished off.

PREPARING NEW WOOD FOR POLISHING.

Scraping.—Woodwork—as it leaves the cabinet-maker's hands—is often unfit for polishing, owing to the presence on its surface of tiny irregularities, such as plane marks and roughnesses, which, although practically unnoticeable when the goods are in "the white" (*i.e.*, unpolished), show up clearly when the work is polished. All these irregularities have to be removed, and the surface of the work subjected to scraping. Cabinet-scrapers are pieces of flat steel, about 1-32nd in. thick, on the blades of which are worked up burr edges, these being sufficiently sharp to scrape off a thin paring from the wood. In order that the corners of the scraper may not dig into the wood and form scratches, they should be slightly rounded. To correctly set a cabinet-scraper requires practice, and unless it is properly sharpened it will be useless for the purpose for which it is required.

In use, the scraper is held obliquely away from the operator at an angle of about 45 degs., an even pressure being exerted and the scraper worked in a forward direction.

Glass-papering.—After the work has been cleaned up with the scraper it is finished off with glass-paper, firstly using No. 1 size, and lastly No. 0. In glass-papering it should be borne in mind that sharp edges are easily spoilt if the work is carried out roughly, and the paper should always be used on a sandpapering block. The paper is cut up in pieces of the required length and wrapped round the cork block in order that a hold can be obtained. In shaped and turned work, the use of the cork has to be dispensed

Staining and Polishing

with, the paper being supported by the fingers, except when shaped corks are available.

Stopping Holes.—In the renovating trade, and also in handling new work, wax will be found practically indispensable for filling up small holes, open joints, or defects in the surface of the work, such as bad knots, etc. Some polishers use ordinary yellow wax or beeswax as a stopping, colouring the wax down with spirit stains to match the surrounding woodwork; but, except in the case of very small cracks, which can be readily filled in by having a piece of wax vigorously rubbed across them, the use of a stopping which requires staining after it is in the wood is liable to result in a patchy appearance. Ordinary wax is not hard enough, and is consequently liable to dent or scratch quickly.

Wax Stopping.—The material known as hard stopping or "Beaumontage" (see page 14), sets hard and solid, and when of the same shade as the woodwork is difficult to distinguish, when polished, from the actual wood. Dealers in polish sell stopping ready-made in a number of colours, such as white, yellow, brown, red, black, green, etc., in imitation of the various hardwoods, the sticks of wax being of a handy size for use; but the purchase of ready-made wax has a drawback in that the range of colours obtainable is limited, whereas if the worker were to make his own—a task which he will not find difficult—he could, by adding various quantities of colouring matter, obtain a variety of shades suitable for any class of job. The groundwork of hard stopping is made up of beeswax, 1 part; powdered resin, 1 part; and orange shellac, 18 parts; the whole being melted together by gentle heat, and care being taken that the mixture does not boil, otherwise it will be liable to chip away from the wood by reason of its thus being rendered too brittle.

In making up a quantity of colours two vessels should be used—one for the stock solution, and the other for adding

Preparing Furniture for French Polishing

the various stains, a sufficient quantity of the stock being transferred to the mixing pot, the colour then being added and the material heated up. If the light-coloured wax be made first, the darker shades can be worked up in the same vessel until the darkest one is arrived at ; but if the black were made up first, it would be impossible to obtain the lighter shades without cleaning out the vessel—a none too pleasant task.

The following stains, which are the powdered dry colours used by painters, etc., should be added to the shellac base for making the various coloured waxes, viz. :—

White Wax.—Add powdered whiting and a little ultramarine blue to check the yellowish tone.

Pale Yellow.—Lemon chrome.

Deep Yellow.—Yellow ochre.

Light Brown.—Yellow ochre and brown umber in equal parts.

Medium Brown.—Brown umber.

Dark Brown.—Brown umber and lamp- or gas-black.

Light Red.—Venetian red and yellow ochre.

Medium Red.—Venetian red.

Dark Red.—Venetian red and gas- or lamp-black.

Dark Reddish Brown.—Venetian red and dark purple brown.

Greens. — Brunswick green — lightened with lemon chrome or yellow ochre, darkened with gas- or lamp-black.

Black.—Gas-black or lamp-black.

Using the Wax.—Provided that the size of the sticks of wax is within reasonable proportions, the shape matters but little. The best way to work them up into convenient shape is to get a couple of pieces of polished iron or brass, about 6 ins. by 9 ins., and, making them warm by immersing in hot water, run a line of the melted wax on one of them, using the other to lay on the stick ; by running the top piece backwards and forwards while both wax and metal are hot,

Staining and Polishing

sticks will be formed which, if not round, will be quite near enough for our purpose.

The wax is used for filling up fissures in the wood, to which it has to be applied very hot. The best method of running the wax in is to grind the roughing from the end of a worn-out file, and, making this hot enough to melt the wax to running point, hold the end of the stick on the smooth portion of the file, allowing the wax to *run* into the hole to be filled up. Take care to keep the file from coming in contact with the wood, or trouble may ensue. After the wax has set firm, which takes but a few seconds, the roughness can be cleaned off with chisel, scraper, and glass-paper. A ready method of applying the wax where perhaps only a small hole has to be filled up is to melt it with the heat of a match or taper, taking care that the wax does not blacken.

In filling up smooth dents with wax, the surface to be covered should have a few holes cut in it with a chisel or bradawl, in order that the stopping may have something to adhere to. In cases where little bits of veneer have become chipped off, a little wax is often found useful, as, instead of having to wait while a fresh piece is put in and becomes dry, the polishing can be proceeded with immediately the wax has been cleaned off. It should be borne in mind that hard stopping is soluble in methylated spirit, and therefore this liquid should not be applied too freely to the surface of the wax.

WOOD-FILLERS AND FILLING IN.

Most woods have a certain openness of grain, which has to be filled in either by the application of a wood-filler or by a plentiful application of polish or varnish. American oak, ash, and elm are typical examples of hungry or open-grained woods, whilst mahogany, walnut, and rosewood have usually but moderately open grain. Birch, satinwood, maple and sycamore may be cited as typical examples

Preparing Furniture for French Polishing

of the close-grained woods. The use of a wood-filler is to fill up the pores of the timber so as to give a smooth, transparent and elastic surface on which the polish may be applied; it also reduces the number of coats of polish required and eliminates a great amount of labour in the rubbing down of the successive coats.

Thus, before we can proceed to polish the work the grain of the wood must be filled up. Of course the wood can be polished without if so desired (see page 57), but walnut and mahogany, oak and ash, should be filled, as their grain is so open. With fine, close-grained woods filling may be dispensed with, but it is advisable to undertake the work for almost every wood.

Fillers.—It is possible now to obtain a number of different ready-prepared wood-fillers which require but the addition of a solvent, such as turpentine or methylated spirit, in order to render them ready for use, the colouring being added by the manufacturers. But by far the most common wood-filler is a mixture of fine plaster-of-paris and water or methylated spirit—the latter for preference, as water has a tendency to raise the grain of the wood, which necessitates a good deal of glass-papering, which in turn tends to rub the filler out of the wood, resulting in a further application being required. The water or methylated spirit and the plaster are better kept apart, dipping the wad of coarse rag—with which the filler should be applied—into the liquid first, and then taking up a sufficient quantity of the powder on the moistened rag. This is better than forming a mixture, as plaster dries very quickly and cannot be remoistened with any degree of certainty as to its being soft and free from lumps, which is very essential in treating the surface of wood, any little scratches showing up plainly when the polishing is done.

The grain-filler, whether it be plaster-of-paris or any other material, should be rubbed in *across* the grain of the wood, any superfluous stuff being wiped off before it has set. When the filler has become hard the surface of the

Staining and Polishing

wood should be lightly glass-papered in order to remove the superfluous filling from the surface. Number o glass-paper is best for this purpose, the movement of the paper being in the direction of the grain of the wood. The colour of plaster being white, it is necessary when dealing with the darker-coloured wood to stain the filling, this being done by adding to the powder certain dry colours, according to the shade required.

The following Colours are required for the various woods :—

Yellow Ochre for oak, ash, elm, satinwood, birch, maple, whitewood, etc.

Brown umber for walnut, teak, amboyna, etc.
Venetian red and a little rose pink for mahogany.
Venetian red and lamp black for rosewood.
Lamp-black or gas-black for ebony.

The worker will be able to judge from experiment the exact quantity of stain he will require to add to his plaster in order to obtain the desired effect, much depending upon the colour of the wood being polished.

Other Fillers.—In addition to ready-made fillers, the following may be noted by those who intend to make their own : Get some plaster-of-paris, saturate a rag with methylated spirits, dip it into the plaster, and rub vigorously across the grain of the wood. Some use finely-crushed whiting mixed with turpentine. In this case add a little pumice powder, which forms the necessary grit. Paraffin or benzoline should never be used as solvents for either whiting or plaster. Another filler is made by taking a portion of either china clay or cornflour, and adding boiled linseed oil, making a mixture of the consistency of putty. Then add a little patent drier, and thin with turpentine. Another alternative is the use of Russian (not "Town") tallow, to which is added whiting or fine plaster, as preferred. The tallow and powder are well mixed, and the filler worked into the pores of the wood, any superfluity being wiped off.

Preparing Furniture for French Polishing

A reliable and inexpensive filler may be made by mixing finely-ground-*dry* whiting and plaster-of-paris in equal proportions. Bring these powders in their dry state to the colour of the wood by mixing with them a little brown umber and rose pink; then thoroughly amalgamate and crush out all the lumps. The whiting used for the purpose should be previously dried, as its natural tendency is to absorb moisture. Mix turpentine with this until the filler acquires the consistency of thick paint, and then add a little gold size to act as a binder.

Plaster-of-paris can now be procured specially finely ground. It is made and used principally for the dental profession, being as fine as flour and used for modelling purposes. If this type of plaster can be obtained it is far superior for the purpose than the rough commercial variety usually sold.

Many other recipes could be given, but those having a vegetable basis such as cornflour are best avoided. Whatever filler is used it should be tinted with the dry colours already mentioned.

The Method of Applying the wood filler is as follows: Paint it liberally on the timber with an ordinary paint brush or piece of old rag. Let it stand for a few minutes until partly dry, when the surface may be rubbed across the grain with an open woven rag or fine canvas, such as upholsterer's scrim. By rubbing across the grain the filler is worked well into the pores, and the surplus amount is then wiped away.

After filling in the work should be set aside, and if possible it should be allowed to stand overnight to enable it to thoroughly harden up the pores of the wood.

DIRECT FILLING WITH POLISH.

Direct Filling with Polish can be substituted for the paste grain-fillers, but this process, while being the best,

Staining and Polishing

proves more costly and takes up more time. To fill with polish direct, the wood should be oiled with raw linseed oil and set aside for an hour or so to bring up the figure of the wood, using the oil sparingly. The wood is then covered with French polish, applied across the grain with a brush or a piece of wadding saturated with polish and covered with a piece of soft rag. The first two or three applications of polish will soak right into the wood, which will now require to be set aside to dry for about a couple of hours. In best work the brush is not used after the first application of polish, the rubber doing the rest. When the first coat has become dry give the wood another coat across the grain, keeping the rubber fairly moist and taking care that the first coat does not pick up. Again set the work aside for a couple of hours, or longer if the polish is tacky.

The next step is to procure some finely-ground pumice-stone powder and a piece of muslin, placing the powder in the muslin and tying up the ends so as to form a bag, in order that the pumice may be pounced on to the polish a little at a time. With the rubber which was used for the first two coats of polish we have now to apply a coat of half polish and half methylated spirit, more spirit being used if the work sticks. The pumice is dusted on the surface of the wood from time to time as it is worked into the grain with the rubber, which should be rubbed lightly with a circular motion, adding polish and spirit to the rubber as it becomes dry. The work should not be continued after the polish shows a tendency to pick up, but should stand aside to dry for a short time. The pumice powder acts as a filler for the grain of the wood and consequently more is required in open woods than in close-grained ones.

When the wood is found to be filled up—a process which may require a goodly number of applications of polish, etc.—the work should be set aside to harden thoroughly, after which it can be well glass-papered until thoroughly smooth, using a few spots of linseed oil on the face of the glass-paper to prevent sticking, or the polish rubbing.

Preparing Furniture for French Polishing

The surface of the wood should now present an absolutely level, dull surface, showing no dents or blemishes.

In the cheaper-class varnished work, wood-fillers are often dispensed with altogether, brown or white hard spirit varnish being applied to the wood with a brush. The varnish, being thick, quickly fills up the pores of the wood, leaving at the same time a glossy surface. Spirit varnishes contain a far greater amount of gum than does ordinary French polish, and as alcohol is used as a solvent they dry off very rapidly, with the result that great care has to be exercised in their application, otherwise they become ropey —*i.e.*, dry off in ridges on the wood.

The Brush used should be that known as a gilder's mop, which is made from short, soft hair. New brushes should be soaked in water for a couple of hours previous to use, in order that the hairs may swell, which will prevent them falling out; but before the brush is used for putting on the varnish or polish it must be thoroughly dry, otherwise the work will suffer. If it is desired to dry the brush off quickly, dip it in methylated spirit for a few minutes, which will have the desired effect of hastening the drying. Once a brush has been used for spirit varnish or French polish, it should not be immersed in water, but washed with methylated spirit. Brushes should be kept in a tin, the same one answering for both rubbers and brushes if sufficiently large.

Varnish and Polish in combination in the proportion of 1 part varnish (brown or white hard spirit) to 3 parts French polish, are also used as a filler, the mixture being laid on with a brush or with a rubber, using no oil in the latter case, but keeping the rubber well moistened in order that the work may not pick up, and taking care not to go over the same ground until the last coat of filler has set a little. When the work is filled in, which may require three or four separate applications, it should be set aside to thoroughly harden, after which it is well ground down with glass-

Staining and Polishing

paper (No 1 first and then No. 0), when it will be ready for bodying-in, a process which is described in the next chapter.

The use of varnish for filling in, although hastening the process of polishing, can always be detected by those who

BOOKCASE OR CHINA CABINET SUITABLE FOR A SHERATON MAHOGANY TREATMENT.

understand the work, as the ultimate finish is never so good or lasting as when the work has been what may be called correctly worked up—that is to say, with the ordinary paste grain-fillers or French polish applied with the rubber.

FRENCH POLISHING

Fatting or Bodying-in—Bodying-up or Working-up
— Colouring — Spiriting — Supporting
Work for Polishing.

THE CONSTITUENTS of French polish vary according to the kind of wood for which the polish is required and also according to the class of work for which it is intended. For light woods, such as holly, sycamore, ash, light oak, satin walnut, etc., white polish should be used. This is made from bleached shellac dissolved in methylated spirits, and is almost colourless. Ordinary polish is made with ordinary orange shellac as a base, other gums, such as tragacanth, mastic, sandarach, etc., being sometimes added for special purposes (see under Shellac, page 39). The ingredients of the ready-made polishes sold by the different manufacturing firms vary according to the maker, some adding certain gums or resins, but shellac is the principal ingredient. Some add one gum to give increased elasticity, while another may be added to harden the film, and so forth. It is therefore safest when ordering ready-made polishes to state the particular kind of polish required.

For a reliable home-made polish the following is recommended, and is suitable for most work: Dissolve 5 or 6 ozs. of shellac in 1 pint of methylated spirits. The shellac will dissolve readily in the spirits without the necessity of heating, an occasional shaking of the bottle or agitating with a stick being all that is required. If it be found necessary to guess the proportions, half fill a bottle with the broken shellac and then fill right up with the spirits.

In French polishing the surface is worked up by subjecting the work to a number of coats, each of which must be thoroughly set before the next one is put on. An article may, however, be started and finished in one day; but if

Staining and Polishing

good and lasting results are desired, a week should be allowed for the work.

Preliminary Oiling.—Some woods are often improved and enriched by oiling. The work is given a thin coating of linseed oil, which brings out the figure of the wood, and to a certain extent darkens and mellows it. The oiling should take place before the polishing, and after the staining when a stain is employed. The oil must be applied very sparingly as too much would prevent the polish from being worked up properly, and might possibly cause the work to subsequently sweat and crack. Mahogany should be oiled with what is termed red oil. This is made by steeping 2 or 3 ozs. of alkanet root in 1 pint of raw linseed oil for twenty-four hours, the proportions varying slightly according to the depth of tone required. Afterwards, when the oil is quite dry, rub down again with glass-paper. The work is then ready for polishing.

The process of French polishing is divided into three stages. The initial stage is termed " fatting-in," " fadding-in " or " slapping-in "; the second stage is known as " building-up " or " bodying-up "; and the final stage is called " spiriting-out."

"BODYING-IN."

By " Bodying-in " or " fatting " (sometimes also called " sizing-in ") is meant the building up on the surface of wood of a film of polish, which, when dry, is worked up to its finished brilliancy. It is not necessary that the film should be thick, but the polish should completely fill the open pores of the wood, which, although they will have been treated with a paste-filler, are nevertheless still absorbent.

In the initial applications of polish, the rubber, which may be made of a wad of cotton-wool having a soft calico or rag covering, or may be a piece of old flannel used without a rag covering, should be used fairly wet with the polish, which latter may be poured into an open china containing-vessel,

French Polishing

and have the wad dipped into it when charging. At first the direction taken with the rubber on the wood should be across the grain, the pressure exerted being light. A common pitfall is the working of the rubber upon an over-wet surface which picks up the film. Care should therefore be exercised, and a part once treated should be allowed a sufficient time to harden before being worked upon again. Within reason, of course, the polish cannot become too hard, and it is better to err on the point of having the work unnecessarily dry rather than to risk picking up the surface.

It is advisable to commence using the rubber in a circular direction as early as possible, gradually working over the entire surface with a combined circular and traversing movement. It will be found inconvenient to do this until the timber has absorbed a certain amount of polish, and this is why we commence our strokes of the rubber backwards and forwards in the first instance.

The polish will be quickly absorbed after the first application of polish, and in a few minutes a second coat can be applied, again working across the grain. The object of this is to fill up the pores better. In this manner give the work three or four coats before setting aside for a few hours. Always allow sufficient time in between the coats for the polish to dry, or it will work up when applying the subsequent coat, and an uneven surface result, which will prove fatal to the making of a good finish. In working it will be found that the wood rapidly absorbs the polish from the rubber, and when the latter has become dry it should be recharged in the manner above described. Do not work at this stage with a dry rubber, but keep it well moistened. The work should now be laid aside for five or six hours, if so much time can be spared; but in any case two hours must be allowed.

On resuming the work it will be noticed that the polish has soaked into the wood a little. Rub it down with very fine glass-paper, and give two more coats across the grain, allowing a few minutes to intervene between each applica-

Staining and Polishing

tion. Use the same rubber as before, provided that it is still soft and that the rag covering has not become clogged. When not in use, these rubbers should be placed in the airtight canister, which, as previously stated (page 48), should be kept for this purpose. A few drops of spirits over the rubbers will further help in keeping them nice and soft. If the covering has become worn or abraded on the sole of the rubber, it must be discarded and a new one procured. After giving the work these two coats, it should be allowed to stand aside again, this time longer than before. If a day can be spared, so much the better.

When it has properly set, paper it down lightly again, but this time put a few drops of linseed oil on the surface of the paper, in order to prevent it scratching the surface or picking up the polish, which will not be too hard. The appearance of the wood will now have changed, and a better body will be noticed. It is well at this point to examine the work for holes, lumps, or any irregularities of surface, which should now be attended to. Any lumps must be brought down with glass-paper, but care must be taken to see that the polish does not get rubbed up in the process. If a small hole is detected this must be filled up by rubbing a bit of wax across it, and the surplus carefully cleaned off. Should the work still appear patchy, owing to an insufficient body of polish, it should receive another coat, or may be two, in the same manner as the previous ones. The fatting-in process is now completed, and when the work has stood a day and become quite hard it will be ready for the second stage, namely bodying-up, or working-up.

In handling Oak and woods of a like open-grained nature, more body will be needed than in dealing, say, with satin walnut, so that the worker must use his own judgment as to the exact amount of bodying-in he allows upon the work in hand. Generally speaking, however, a good film should be worked up without the use of oil, not by continued application of the rubber to the surface, but by going over it at intervals, so that the film may harden off. To

French Polishing

avoid lumpiness, it is desirable that the wood be gone over from time to time during the process with fine glass-paper, upon the face of which should be sprinkled a few drops of raw linseed oil. A little oil rubbed over the wood with a piece of rag previous to polish being used has the effect of toning down colour and enriching figure; but after oiling, the work should be set aside for a while before the polishing is commenced.

BODYING-UP OR WORKING-UP.

With the second stage of French polishing, termed working-up or bodying-up, great care must be exercised, as ultimate success depends very largely upon this process. The surface of the work should be glass-papered down until quite flat and dead; no shine should appear. Dust carefully, and commence by wiping the work over with a rag dipped in linseed oil; but only a very small quantity should be put on, as it is only to prevent the rubber from sticking to the last coat of polish. An old rubber is better than a new one for bodying-up, so that the one used for fatting-in should be used, provided it has been kept soft and clean. Or a new rubber made of wadding—shaped on its sole, and worked up to the shape shown on page 48 (Fig. 16)—may be used instead. The rubber is covered with a piece of fine soft rag, which must be quite free from creases where it covers the sole of the rubber, and the ends of which should be pulled up to the top of the rubber and there wrapped round, so as to be out of the way. Fig. 17 (page 66) illustrates the method of holding the rubber.

Charge the rubber with the same polish as was used previously, and in the same manner, but this time put a few spots of oil on the surface of the rubber with the finger-tips. Give the work a good coat all over, moving the rubber round with a circular motion and not in straight long sweeps. No precise rules can be laid down regarding

Staining and Polishing

the working of the rubber, as much depends upon the size and character of the wood. But the path of the rubber should somewhat follow the direction of the lines shown in Fig. 18, which can, however, be varied a little at the discretion of the polisher. In starting do not bang the rubber on to the wood, but work it on gently, and in finishing take it off gradually, or the place will show where the rubbing has terminated abruptly. *Never allow the*

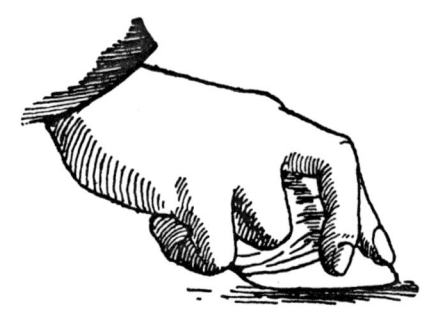

FIG. 17.—HOW TO HOLD THE RUBBER.

rubber to stand on the work, but always keep it in motion when in contact with a polished surface.

A little polish goes a long way, and the beginner must carefully avoid making the rubber too wet. It should not be more than fairly moist. It is wrong to suppose that the more polish used the quicker will the result be obtained, as too much will inevitably cause the surface to be ridgy and irregular, instead of smooth and even. On the other hand, the rubber must not be worked too dry, but should contain just sufficient polish to keep it from dragging. In practice the worker will find that the rubber soon begins to drag, and when it gets so that it cannot be worked properly across the surface of the wood a few drops of raw linseed oil should be applied to the sole of the rubber to make it go easier. It may sometimes be due to the

French Polishing

want of polish, or to polish which is too thick, and this will probably be the case if a new rubber is being used, so that a recharge should be made instead of applying oil. Remember that the oil is only used as a lubricant and forms no part of the polish. Too much of it is fatal to the work, and only when absolutely necessary should it be used. The oil comes up in the form of smears, all traces of which have got to be removed in the spiriting-out or

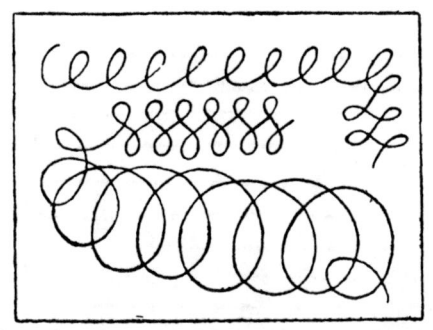

FIG. 18.—SHOWING MOVEMENTS OF RUBBER.

finishing process. If on examining the face of the rubber it appears shiny, too much oil is being used. Hence, the more sparingly it is used the better.

Many workers prefer poppy oil to linseed oil for lubricating the polishing rubber, especially those who use the acid finish.

After a coat has been laid on and the polish begun to set, get the rubber to work again, and go over the surface gently until a semi-lustrous surface is worked up, taking care not to work on the surface long enough to get the under polish wet and liable to pick up. When the polish feels to be pulling on the rubber, give the work a rest for a little time, and go over it again when it has begun to set. It is much better when several articles have to be polished at once, as the operator can then pass from one

Staining and Polishing

to the other, and allow sufficient time for each to set before giving a further coat; besides, there is no time wasted in waiting.

The number of times the work requires to be bodied will depend on circumstances. The fine, close-grained woods will not require so many applications as the more open-grained ones, but as a general rule three bodies, or at the outside four, will be found sufficient for a good job.

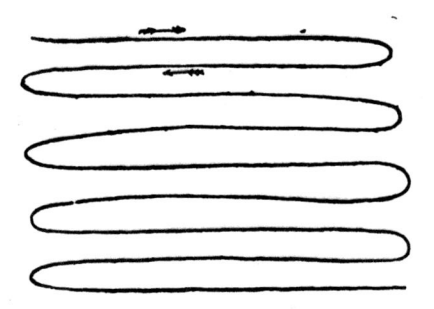

FIG. 19.—INCORRECT MOVEMENT OF RUBBER.

An interval of at least one day should elapse between the successive bodies, the chief object of waiting being to let them sink in as much as they will. This will, however, be regulated according to circumstances, but it should be borne in mind that the longer the time allowed between coats the better will the finished surface be. In any case the polish must be set before another coat is put on, or there will be danger of working it up again.

When resuming the work it should receive a slight rubbing down with spent glass-paper. If no paper can be found which has been previously used, and only the new is at hand, rub two pieces together to remove the sharpness and modify the cutting power, so as to prevent scratching the polish. The bodying process may be considered com-

French Polishing

plete when the polish no longer seems to sink in, even after a few days' lapse. There will be a slight gloss on the surface, but it will be streaky and full of rubber marks which will show very distinctly. All these marks will be removed later on.

If, however, the polish has a lumpy or stringy appearance it must be levelled down at this stage. To do this effectively, the pounce bag (described on page 44) must be called into requisition. Give the work a few taps with the bag, and proceed to polish as before, but adding spirits instead of polish to the rubber. Apply also a few spots of oil to the work. A new rubber must not be used for this purpose, but one well charged with the polish, to the extent of almost being clogged up with it. The spirits will work it out, and leave the rubber soft and pliable. Do not attempt to use the pumice with thick polish, or the movement of the rubber will gather the pumice into a heap. Repeat the process several times, giving the work an occasional tap with the pumice bag, adding a little spirits to the rubber and a few drops of oil to enable the rubber to work freely. After the bodying-in is completed the work should be set aside for a day or so, and covered carefully over with sheets to keep out the dust. The work is then ready for the final polishing, termed spiriting-out, unless colouring up or matching has to be done.

COLOURING.

Colouring up the work is almost always necessary, even in the best selected timber, and to obtain the exact shade everything depends upon the skill of the workman *plus* a good eye for colour.

The method generally in use is to mix one part of polish and two parts of spirits, and strain this liquid through a combination of suitably coloured pigments. In this case a rag containing a little dry powdered vandyke brown, bismarck brown, and a little vegetable- or lamp-black

Staining and Polishing

will be found suitable. This will give the polish any desired tint by altering the proportion of dry colours and the number of times the polish is strained through the powders.

Take a fine camel hair or sable mop brush and dip it into the colour; work out any excess of the liquid on the side of the pot, and literally paint over the light portions, working the brush with the grain of the wood. Do not attempt to go over the same place twice until thoroughly dry; it is much better to get the desired shade by two or even three applications of the colour than by applying one coat of thick, dark, patchy polish.

When dry, skim the surface of the work with an old piece of No. 0 glass-paper to take off the dust nibs, bearing in mind that the paper must be used very lightly.

The required colour having been obtained, it is necessary to fasten it, and this is accomplished by taking the same brush and giving the whole surface one coat of thin white polish, using the brush similarly as when colouring up. The surface should now be allowed to harden up for some hours, and on taking up the work it will be required to again skim the surface of the work with old glass-paper and proceed to again body up the work.

The number of times the work will be required to be bodied up depends upon the texture and porosity of the timber; three or four times in all is rarely exceeded.

For further hints on colouring see page 90, under MATCHING-UP.

SPIRITING.

Spiriting-out is the operation by which the gloss is put on the body previously applied. Bodying is the important process for getting a good film of polish on to the work and so making it durable; but spiriting is most important with regard to finish. It is this operation which has to remove all the smears and rubber marks, and present that beautiful surface which is the distinguishing feature of

French Polishing

French polish. Failure in spiriting-out will to a considerable extent render previous efforts vain, and it is at this stage that more skill is required than in any other portion of the polisher's art, excepting perhaps the process of darkening and staining, with which every good polisher should be acquainted. The beginning of the process of spiriting-out is really bodying-in, and the end is spiriting. The two processes really merge one into the other, there being no abrupt break as between fatting and bodying.

A Spirit Rubber is made from cotton wadding which has been dipped in spirits. All excess moisture is squeezed out, and it is a good plan to make the rubber a day before it is required and place it overnight in an airtight tin. When using the spirit rubber, not less than two thicknesses of rag should be used to cover it; needless to add, the rag must be clean, soft and free from lint. A nice old well-washed pocket-handkerchief is as good as anything that can be obtained.

When spiriting-out, the beginner can hardly err by using too little spirits; the rubber should simply be moist and damp. The path of the rubber should be the same as when bodying-up, and pressure should at first be light and gradually increased as the spirit dries out of the rubber. The direction of the rubber, when just on the point of finishing, is in the direction of the grain of the wood.

Many polishers prefer to dispense with the spirit rubber, and, after gradually thinning down the last bodying rubber until nearly all marks have vanished, they take a piece of nice soft cloth, fold it in the form of a pad, sprinkle a little spirits on the palm of the left hand, and dab the pad upon this so as to slightly damp the surface. The pad is used backwards and forwards on the work until the final burnishing is completed. Another method of finishing work, especially where the ends of sideboards, etc., are not required to be spirited out, is known as "stiffing-up."

Stiffing-up.—After thinning down the last body

Staining and Polishing

rubber, a new rubber is taken and charged with "toppings" and this is worked out fairly dry in the direction of the grain. Toppings is obtained by pouring off the semi-transparent fluid which accumulates on the top of white polish, after it has stood a few days in the bottle. The toppings should be carefully poured off the polish and bottled separately. It is a much superior and more lasting finish than can be obtained by glaze. Toppings can be treated with the spirit pad with very good results, but on no account use oil when applying toppings or glaze.

Glaze, dealt with in another section (page 77), is prepared by crushing gum benzoin and dissolving it in spirits; it is used for finishing small articles which cannot be spirited out, such as brackets and chair rails, etc. Glaze should be carefully strained through fine rag and kept bottled ready for use. The method of applying glaze is by using it on a rubber or sponge; it is applied fairly wet on to the polished surface, the latter of course being free from oil before its application. Glazing is nothing more or less than spreading a thin varnish on a body of polish; whereas spiriting-out is burnishing up the body proper.

REFINED OR ACID FINISH.

The Refined or Acid Method of finishing polished work is principally used abroad, although many British polishers now use the same method. Instead of spiriting-out the work with a spirit rubber, it is treated as follows: Pounce Vienna chalk (not French chalk as suggested by some writers; chemically speaking, they are different substances) liberally over the polished surface, and have at hand a suitable earthenware or glass vessel containing a mixture of sulphuric acid diluted with from eight to ten parts of water. Dip the palm of the perfectly clean hand in the acid solution and proceed to rub the chalk with a circular or straight motion, applying sufficient of the acid solution so as to make the chalk become a creamy paste;

French Polishing

continue with the rubbing until the chalk dries off in fine powder. In making up this solution, the acid should be added to the water drop by drop. The acid has the effect of hardening the film of shellac, whilst the chalk brings away any oil that may be on the surface of the work. Instead of using the bare hand some workers prefer a small piece of soft chamois leather.

Pianos.—Another method, used to finish pianos, is by means of clarified ox-gall, used on a piece of soft rag after the spiriting-out or acid finish has been completed. A bladder containing ox-gall is purchased from the butcher, and the ox-gall is filtered as follows : Take a large clean jar and fold clean white blotting-paper so as to make a funnel; place into the funnel about one pennyworth of crushed bone charcoal and allow the ox-gall to be filtered through it. Apply the filtered ox-gall immediately after the acid finish or spiriting-out process has been completed.

SUPPORTING WORK FOR POLISHING.

Polishing is a trade which can be taken up by one-handed, one-armed or otherwise disabled men. Such workers require to adopt methods of holding and supporting work whilst polishing, and in any case it is often an advantage for the able-bodied polisher to adopt some such methods of support. For instance, at Fig. 20 the method of polishing turned work, such as sideboard pillars, etc., is shown. Two small blocks with V-shaped notches in them are kept for this particular purpose, and the turned pins on the pillar rest in these notches, thus allowing the pillar to be revolved with one hand whilst the polish rubber is applied with the other. If the turned work has no wooden pins or dowels the difficulty is overcome by driving a 3-in. round wire nail into each end of the work to act as temporary supports. The small supporting brackets are made in pairs of suitable heights to suit all classes of general work, say, one pair 3 ins. high, one pair 5 ins. high, and one pair

Staining and Polishing

7 ins. high. They are made out of rough wood with the upright piece screwed to the base.

Temporary Fixing of Panels.—Flat panels are held down upon a temporary board kept for the purpose by large-headed $\frac{5}{8}$-in. tacks as shown at A., Fig. 21. The heads of the

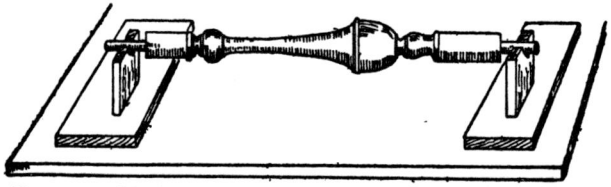

FIG. 20.—METHOD OF SUPPORTING TURNED WORK FOR POLISHING.

tacks are driven well down below the surface to be polished, and any small defect they make in the edge of the panel is covered by the rebate of the door frame. One frequently sees four or five panels fixed on one long board by the above method during the polishing process. Straight and curved

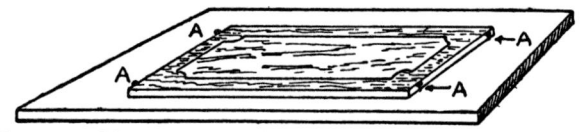

FIG. 21.—METHOD OF HOLDING PANELS FOR POLISHING. A, A INDICATE $\frac{5}{8}$-IN. LARGE-HEADED TACKS.

lengths of mouldings are held down to a temporary board in a similar manner, or by temporary screws of suitable length being put in from the underside.

Holding Drawers, Boxes and Coffins.—Drawer fronts, boxes, coffins, etc., are supported by screwing two battens at a suitable distance apart, as shown at Fig. 22, and laying the drawer or box on these supports. This allows the worker, after bodying-up one face of a box, to lift it off the battens and replace the box with another of its sides (or ends)

French Polishing

uppermost, thus enabling the worker to proceed without waiting for the opposite side (or end) to dry and harden up.

Handling small Shapings and Brackets.—A method of holding small shelf brackets and similar shapings that are to be polished on three sides is shown at Fig. 23. A

FIG. 22.—METHOD OF SUPPORTING DRAWERS, BOXES, ETC.

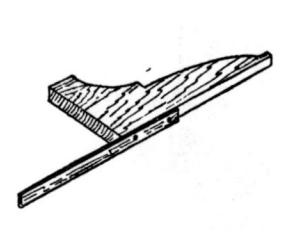

FIG. 23.—METHOD OF HOLDING BRACKETS.

FIG. 24.—MOUNTING APPLIED CARVINGS.

small narrow piece of wood is screwed with two $\frac{5}{8}$-in. screws to the unpolished edge, thus forming a convenient handling piece.

Polishing applied Carvings.—For mounting and polishing applied carvings, such as are used on Louis XV.

Staining and Polishing

cabinets, etc., the usual plan is to put a few spots of thin glue on the carving and press the carving on to a piece of newspaper; then glue the underside of the newspaper

FIG. 25.—HOLDING BOTTLE WITH ONE HAND.

down on to the temporary board as at Fig. 24. When the polishing is completed a thin dinner-knife blade is inserted under the carving to release it.

FIG. 26.—USING BOTTLE (INVERTED).

Single-handed Polishers.—The writer, after making one or two experiments, finds that a man with only one hand can successfully charge his rubber with polish by using a small-sized medicine bottle, around the top and bottom of which are wrapped two bandages of rag or tape as shown in Figs. 25 and 26.

GLAZING

Glazing—Dry-Shining—Egg-shell and Dull Polishing—Spirit Enamelling—Treatment of Carved Work

WOODWORKERS frequently wish to try a quick method of polishing, and when this is necessary a special process, termed Glazing, is resorted to as a substitute for spiriting-out. The cheapness lies in the saving of labour rather than in the cost of material. The gum used for making glaze is more expensive than that which is used in making ordinary polish. It is simply a means of obtaining the effect of spiriting easily and quickly though the finish is not so good or so durable as when the spiriting is done. There is not that fine, beautiful lustre which is obtained by the ordinary process of finishing. Glazing is, however, very convenient occasionally, and for some things has an advantage over spiriting, and therefore may be classed among the ordinary processes of polishing. It is particularly useful for carvings, turned work, moulding, and such parts as cannot readily be got at with the rubber, in which case the brush is used. On such places as these it is usually employed even on what is considered good-class work. But on low-grade work it almost always displaces spiriting, both for flat and carved surfaces. It is not to be recommended for broad, plain surfaces, however, as its manner of application renders it difficult to obtain an even surface.

Glaze may be bought ready-made, but it may easily be made at home. It is exactly like making the ordinary polish, except that gum benzoin is used in place of shellac, the proportions being about the same. Dissolve about 6 ozs. of the best gum benzoin in 1 pint of methylated spirits and let it stand. Glaze improves by keeping, and is really not fit for use when newly made. Sometimes other gums are added, but this is all that is necessary for the

Staining and Polishing

average glaze. A brush is also sometimes used for plain surfaces, but a rubber is better. This rubber is made in the same way as that used for ordinary French polishing.

The work must have been bodied up, and the stage reached where "half-and-half" is being used before the glaze is applied. The rubber should be made wetter than for ordinary polishing, but not so wet as to drip. It should, however, be wet enough to allow of a fair amount of the glaze to be left on the wood with only a very slight pressure. Glaze is, as it were, *painted on* rather than rubbed into the work, no friction taking place. To apply it, dip the rubber into the glaze, and wipe over the work quickly and lightly and in the direction of the grain. Do not go over the same place twice until the previous coat is quite dry. The coats may be repeated in the same manner until a satisfactory gloss has been obtained. When a brush is employed the glaze is applied in exactly the same way as a varnish. A mixture of equal quantities of French polish and glaze may be used with advantage with a brush.

The Gloss may be improved by lightly passing a rubber, charged with spirits only, over it. This should be done with great care, as the glaze may be washed off. To obtain a dull surface add about one-third of sandarac to the glaze solution. The rubber must not be used saturated for this, but should simply be damp.

Wide Surfaces.—There is a danger in glazing plain wide surfaces, owing to the fact that the way in which it is applied makes it extremely difficult for unskilled hands to do the work without creating ridges on the surface. This applies more particularly to the use of the rubber than to the use of the brush, though there is a danger connected with both. Practice will overcome it to a great degree. When ridges have been left on the surface, moisten a swab rubber with a very little spirits and the slightest trace of oil, and go over the glazed surface very lightly, varying the direction of the rubbing, and working in much the same manner as

Glazing

for spiriting-out. In this way all ridges will be worked down, and a smooth even surface obtained with a tolerably good gloss.

The Rubber.—To make the swab rubber, get a fair-sized piece of clean rag, and fold it up into a swab or pad, somewhat resembling the form of an ordinary rubber. But no wadding is used with this one. It is simply a loose form of rag rubber, slightly moistened with spirits only, and rubbed over the work with very little pressure.

DRY-SHINING.

Dry-shining is the term applied to a very cheap and expeditious process of polishing. It is, perhaps, the crudest and simplest way of finishing woodwork by the use of shellac and methylated spirits. After French polishing proper has been thoroughly mastered this process is simplicity itself. As the same ingredients as are used in the making of French polish are also used for this purpose, and the same rubbers are used, it is distinctly a process of French polishing. It is, however, the nearest approach to varnishing that polishers practise, the difference lying in the fact that it is (or should be) applied with a rubber instead of a brush.

Although dry-shining may appear to be somewhat like glazing, yet it is different. It is not, like glazing, a substitute for the tedious process of spiriting-out, and no one must expect to get a higher degree of finish on their work by its adoption.

When a glaze finish is employed, the work is got up in a proper manner; that is, the wood is filled, fatted-in, and bodied up, just as if a really first-class finish was going to be made. But for dry-shining the whole of the treatment to which the work is subjected from beginning to end is of a cheaper character. The pores of the wood are not filled up with a proper filling, but are left open, the polish being allowed to sink in as it may. Two or three coats of ordinary

Staining and Polishing

polish are applied as quickly as possible, and no attempt is made to body the work up to a proper condition. It is, however, executed in much the same manner as bodying-up, but it is not necessary to take the same precautions to get up a good body. It would, perhaps, be more correct to say that the work is wiped over with the polish rubber, not much trouble being taken with it, or it would make the work almost as hard as that secured by ordinary French polishing.

When the bodying has been done to the satisfaction of the polisher, and is quite dry, charge the rubber again with the polish, but have it wetter this time than it was when used for bodying, and wipe over the work in the direction of the grain of the wood, much in the same manner as when directed for glazing. The rubber may be worked backwards and forwards until dry, but as it will drag when becoming dry, and as no oil must be used as a lubricant in this process, it is a better plan to let the polish deposited by each rub dry before going over the same place again.

It must be understood that a high degree of finish cannot be obtained by this method, but it is certainly better than no polish at all. Its chief merit lies in the fact that it can be done expeditiously and therefore cheaply, and it is useful for finishing inside parts of cabinets and similar furniture, as well as for objects which are never placed near the eye.

EGG-SHELL GLOSS—OR DULLING POLISHED WORK.

We here describe the manner of obtaining that dull finish, sometimes called " egg-shell gloss," which is so characteristic of ebonised work and most antique furniture. It also often happens that certain woods show up to better advantage when not highly polished.

For instance, with a well-polished surface the reflection of light may make it necessary for one to stand directly opposite the article to perceive the full beauty of its markings or figure. This is obviated to a great extent if the

Glazing

surface is dull. The work is got up in the usual way to a bright surface, a good body of polish being laid on. It is at that stage where either the spirit or glaze rubber should play its part to give the final brightness that the dulling takes place.

The work must be allowed to stand until thoroughly hard before it is rubbed down, or an even dulness will not be obtained. Procure a piece of felt (a portion of an old felt hat will do, provided it is freed from dust and made clean) or a piece of cloth or rag. Felt is the better material to employ, however, and should be used if possible. Have by you a dish of raw oil, and a quantity of either pumice powder, fine emery powder, or rotten stone. Dip the felt into the oil, then into the pumice or emery, and rub well all over the work with a circular motion. Apply a gentle but firm pressure while rubbing, not too light, or the results will be decidedly slow, but on the other hand not too heavy, or the surface will be damaged. The rubbing must be distributed equally over the entire surface, and the felt kept well supplied with the oil and powder. A well-worn sash tool or shoe brush may be used to rub the powder and oil into the corners, quirks or carvings.

The operation must be repeated until the whole of the work is one uniform dulness; then wipe perfectly clean with a quantity of clean, soft rag. Finally, wipe over with a rag just damped with benzoin. The work may be dulled with the brush and pumice powder only, but in this case the brushing must be in the same direction as the grain of the wood. Supposing, for instance, that a door has to be dulled with the brush. The top and bottom rails must be done without brushing on to the stiles more than one can help. The same thing applies when doing the stiles. Do not forget to equalise the dulling. For the corners of mouldings, etc., use a smaller brush. Pumice powder is most generally used, but sometimes emery powder is used because of its greater cutting power. When properly done the result is a semi-lustrous finish, which

Staining and Polishing

has a beauty and charm after years of wear and constant cleaning.

Interior Parts of Furniture.—It should be noted that polishing the interior parts of furniture has a very valuable effect in prolonging its life, as by preserving the inside from the effects of the atmosphere the unequal shrinkage or expansion which would otherwise result is prevented. A drawer or cupboard door which has a tendency to stick in damp weather can often be cured by thoroughly drying and then coating the unpolished parts with polish as described, taking care, of course, to see that the film of polish does not itself cause jamming.

Small Mouldings and Turned Parts may be given a coat of varnish thinned with a little polish, and laid on with a camel-hair brush after the work is first bodied in. It should be papered down the same as flat surfaces, using half-worn-out No. 0 glass-paper. This will help to make all the work of an even thickness, which can only be otherwise obtained by constant practice.

Carving may be similarly treated, and when a good surface has been obtained, finished with a thin coat of varnish, or by glazing, which must be done as follows: Mix 1 oz. of benzoin and 1 gill of methylated spirit. When dissolved, strain it through a piece of close rag; make a small rubber, which must be kept for this purpose only; fill the rubber with the glaze, and wipe over lightly and quickly, care being taken not to go over the work a second time until the first is quite dry. Mouldings, turned work, and narrow, flat surfaces may be finished in the same manner.

Carvings that are to be finished dull and with the grain open will require very particular attention; they may be oiled or stained with the other parts, but in filling in flat surfaces care must be taken that none of the filler gets into the carving, or the work when finished will have a very unsatisfactory appearance. They must, after staining

Glazing

or oiling, be given a coat of polish with a camel-hair brush, and, if necessary, a second coat tinted with a little red polish. When dry, brush with a hog's-hair brush and rub with a piece of coarse rag; this will make them quite smooth. If required to be half bright give two or three coats of polish, and when dry rub with a piece of coarse rag only.

Carvings are also dull polished with a stiff nail-brush and beeswax. The nail-brush is rubbed vigorously on a lump of beeswax and then the brush is applied to the carvings in a similar manner; repeated applications are, of course, required to give the desired result. This method is particularly useful on fumed oak carvings.

SPIRIT ENAMELLING.

The methods of finishing wood in various colours, so as to allow of a French-polish finish, will be of interest to those who have already acquired some degree of proficiency. We will call it enamelling, though it must not be confounded with the ordinary ready-made enamels which are sold at all painters' and decorators' shops. The latter are enamels with an oil basis, and are not suitable for finishing with French polish. Of course, these are not usually intended to precede the application of any other material, but are considered to be a finish in themselves. They are all right for certain classes of work, but do not produce "spirit enamelling." What we are dealing with now is a different kind of enamel, being colour ground in spirit instead of oil. This renders it capable of being finished by French-polish methods. Another advantage is that it dries quickly, whereas oil enamels take about a day to dry, and even then are not quite hard.

As enamelling is like painting, in that it totally obscures the grain of the wood and presents an even, solid body of colour, it follows that such work is always done upon the cheaper and plainer varieties of wood, such as pine.

Staining and Polishing

It would be foolish to waste the more valuable woods for this kind of work. If the article is to be finished white, make a mixture of glue size and whiting; or instead of glue size clear parchment size may be used. Either of these sizes may be obtained from a picture-framer. Mix into a moderately thin paste, and apply two or three coats with a bristle brush, allowing each coat sufficient time to dry before the next is applied. This acts as a filler, and also helps to build up a smooth surface of the colour required.

Now make a transparent polish from 2 ozs. bleached shellac, ½ oz. benzoin, 1 oz. juniper, and 1 pint methylated spirits. Well digest the whole by the aid of a warm bath, and when cold carefully decant off until entirely free from residue; then warm again, and strain thoroughly. Next procure some finely-crushed flake white, and well mix into the polish. This should be allowed to stand a little while, and be carefully strained before use, either by the help of a very fine sieve or some very fine muslin. When ready, apply several coats with a camel-hair brush, repeating the coats until a solid appearance is obtained. Smooth down gently with worn glass-paper, and then mix some of the body colour with transparent varnish, and give the work two coats of this. When quite hard rub down again, this time with much care to avoid rubbing through to the wood.

A colourless varnish may be made from 5 ozs. of clean yellow resin, 1 oz. gum sandarac, and ½ pint of spirits of turpentine, well digested in a warm bath. Or dissolve 2 ozs. of gum mastic and 6 ozs. of gum sandarac in 4 ozs. of clear Venice turpentine. But the polishes and the varnishes can be obtained ready-made if so desired. After the work has received the two coats just mentioned and has been rubbed down, it is ready for French polishing in the ordinary way.

Colours.—If the colour is required to be cream, just add the tiniest bit of chrome to the tinted polish and varnish,

Glazing

and instead of using transparent polish use brown, made from orange shellac. Otherwise proceed in exactly the same manner as directed for white. Similarly, other colours may be built up by using dry pigments of the desired hue, and using brown polish instead of transparent. But it might be well to add that if using a green, especially if it is a bright green, the use of brown polish is liable to turn it yellower and destroy its brightness. Therefore it may be taken as an axiom that, when light or very bright colours are to be used, transparent polish and varnish should be employed; whilst if the colours are to be dark and subdued, brown polish may be used.

For dark colours the groundwork should be built up with dry colours mixed with the glue, instead of whiting as recommended for white and cream. Dry colours can be obtained in almost any shade, and may be intermixed to get any required colour. Obtain, however, pigments of good quality for this purpose, or the results may be disappointing. Spirit enamels present a surface more readily adaptable for purposes of decorative ornament, such as gilding, hand-painting, or transfer decorations. Spirit enamels can also be used with advantage for painting decorative shields on cardboard or wood for bazaars and carnivals, etc., where quick-drying colours are essential. A dead surface may be obtained by either thinning out the last coat with methylated spirits and the addition of a little raw linseed oil, or by dulling with pumice powder as previously directed.

Another Plan which may be adopted is to mix the body colour with half polish and half spirits, laying on coat after coat until a solid appearance is obtained. In this manner two or more distinctive colours may be laid on the same article, either side by side or underneath each other after the manner of scumbling. By the latter method some really beautiful effects can be got, especially if bright colours are used. We touched on the subject of scumbling in the sections on staining. When these colours are dry,

Staining and Polishing

smooth down and apply one coat of clear spirit varnish. After again smoothing down the work is ready for French polishing.

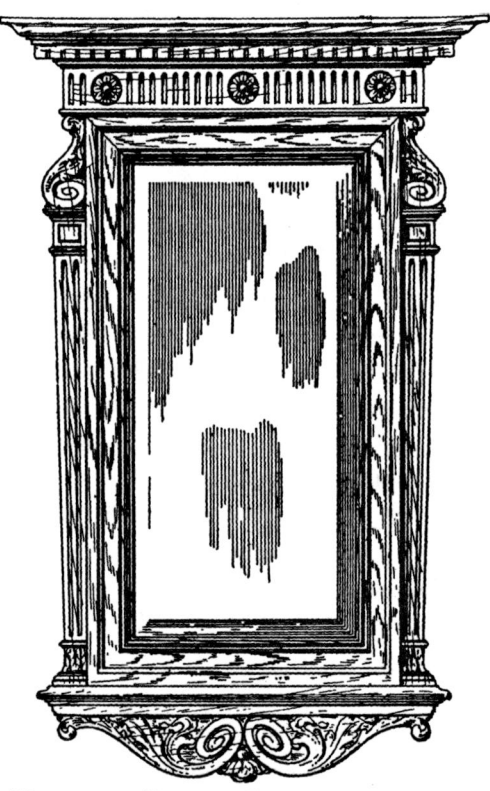

MIRROR OR PICTURE FRAME—ADAM STYLE.

Picture-frames lend themselves splendidly to this class of work, as also do small articles of furniture, knicknacks, etc. If frames are being done, the picture and the glass must be removed and the frame well dusted.

MATCHING AND IMPROVING

Removing Old Polish—Re-polishing Old Furniture

BEFORE dealing with the re-polishing of old furniture, some hints may be offered on the matching-up and improving of woodwork generally.

When the principles and processes of French polishing already explained have been fully mastered, it is a comparatively easy matter to give to a plain piece of wood a level and lustrous surface; and when to this is added a knowledge of staining, derived from the section devoted to that subject, the polisher may present a fair imitation of any given wood with but little labour. This, however, applies more particularly to inferior and lighter woods, the object being to make them represent more expensive and darker kinds.

Matching.—Stains have sometimes to be used in polishing; though in this case the stain is usually mixed with the polish, and applied in a different manner from ordinary staining. The process is termed "matching-up," and refers to the treatment of woods which in their natural state vary considerably in colour over one surface or one article of furniture. The darker parts may need lightening, or the lighter parts need darkening, but it is the usual thing to take the latter course and aim at a uniform colour by making the wood darker. The process needs some practice to master, and a good eye for colour is also needed.

Apart from the natural unevenness of colour in the darker woods, it is sometimes difficult to obtain a uniform tone when staining white woods. Hence the necessity of understanding matching and improving. A practical French polisher does not worry about getting the exact tone by means of stain alone, because he knows how far coloured filling, red oil, dyed polish and varnish, etc., will assist him in attaining it. The importance of this cannot be over-estimated, as it may save much vexation and

Staining and Polishing

worry when endeavouring to obtain a particular result by means of stains alone.

Oiling.—First may be mentioned oiling as a means of darkening and improving the tone of the work. The oil generally used by polishers is raw linseed oil, although some prefer others, such as almond, sweet oil, etc. Raw linseed is quite sufficient, however, and no other oil need be stocked, unless it be for some exceptional kind of work. Few of the darker kinds of woods show up without toning of some sort, and the oiling has a very softening effect. It may be mentioned that dark woods show up considerably better with oiling than do the lighter ones. Where staining is to be done also it must be done previous to oiling; for if the latter is done first, then the oil will to a certain extent have filled the pores of the wood and have rendered it impossible for the stain to soak in as it should.

The work having been cleaned up, stained and filled in, it is then ready to receive a thin coating of the oil, which may be applied with a thin piece of soft cotton rag. It should be applied sparingly, as an excess would prevent the polish from being worked up properly, and may cause it to subsequently sweat and crack. Though the oil darkens the wood, its principal use is to bring out the figure. In the different varieties of mahogany, that which is termed bay mahogany is much lighter than either Spanish or Honduras, and is but slightly affected by the application of oil to its surface; but the latter varieties, which are reddish-brown in colour, quickly change to a much deeper tone when oiled.

For use on mahogany, however, the red oil is best. This is made in the following manner: Make a muslin bag, and put in about a quarter of a pound of alkanet root. Put a pint of raw linseed oil into a jar or other vessel, and suspend the muslin bag in the oil. Leave it to stand for one or more days, and when the oil is properly coloured strain into a bottle and cork up. After oiling, the work should really stand for twelve or fifteen hours before

Matching and Improving

polishing. Many polishers add a little turpentine to the red oil to assist evaporation and to facilitate the spreading of same. Both English and American oak are improved by oiling, but, as they are invariably finished light, uncoloured oil should of course be used. Walnut is another wood which has varying darkening properties when oiled. In this, as in mahogany, the lighter varieties are little affected by the oil, whilst that which possesses a marked black figuring tones down quickly with the application.

Stained Polish.—For matching-up we shall require a few dyes, soluble in spirit, and also a few dry-powder colours. These colours should include yellow ochre, Venetian red, vegetable-black, lamp-black, burnt umber, vandyke brown, greens, lemon chrome, orange chrome, blues, etc. It is better and more convenient to have these colours mixed up with polish in separate bottles, the polish being fairly weak—in the proportion of three parts of methylated spirit to one part polish. Some colour will have to be left in the dry state. The stained polish must not be too dark and opaque, otherwise the grain of the wood will be hidden, and the work appear more as if it were painted or enamelled. It should not be used all through the polishing, but only in the primary coats. It may be applied either by the means of rubber or brush. The latter is the more popular method, a camel-hair brush, like a gilder's mop, being the one employed.

Sap Colouring.—To colour up a piece of sap or other light portion on walnut, go over the wood several times with the polish rubber to prevent the grain from rising, and then saturate a small tuft of wadding with three parts spirits to one part polish. On this wadding place a small quantity of vandyke brown or burnt umber; mix well and carefully wipe over the light portions, thinning out with spirits if too dark, picking up a little more colour if not dark enough, and adding a little black if required.

On large, flat surfaces coloured polish may be used with

Staining and Polishing

advantage, but for small work it would be better to take a small tuft of wadding and wet it with the polish, the latter being in the proportion as stated above. With this take up a little yellow ochre and a trace of umber or vandyke brown. Press the wadding well on the back of an old piece of glass-paper, to equalise the polish and colour, and mix them well. It is better to try it first on an odd corner of the work, and if too dark thin out with spirits, while if not quite dark enough pick up more colour or go over it twice.

Having obtained the right shade, apply lightly with a straight or wavy motion as desired. The colours just given are useful for oak, but the manner of treatment is suitable for any wood. For large, plain surfaces it is a safer plan to mix the colours up in the polish, and apply with the brush; or, if a wavy grain is required, apply the polish with a feather. This prevents patchiness. After laying on the stain, a few minutes must be allowed for it to set; then glass-paper lightly, and fasten the stain with a thin coat of polish. In a further ten minutes or so the work will be ready for polishing.

Colouring-up.—This has already been dealt with on page 69. A stain much used for this kind of work is chroma. This is simply a solution of bichromate of potash (2 ozs. of the crystal in a pint of water make a medium strength), and is a yellow stain of a soft and pleasing character. Spanish or Honduras mahoganies that are required darker than their natural colour may be toned down with chroma. It has also a very enriching effect upon walnut. In matching-up satin walnut the polisher must use judgment, for the work can hardly be regarded as mechanical. The stain must depend upon the colour of the lighter parts and of the darker parts with which they are to be matched. Generally, a little weak brown stain will do what is required. When necessary it can be altered slightly in colour by the addition of other pigments, according to the tints required. A red stain and dry black may

Matching and Improving

be used both separately and in combination for the matching up of rosewood.

In cases where oak is required to be made dark, a sufficient number of coats of chroma solution can be applied, which will give a rich colour to the work without spoiling the figure of the wood. If a less prominent effect is desired, an application of vandyke brown will colour the material down, but will in a measure obliterate the figuring. Black oak—more correctly the imitation of black oak—should not be dead black in colour, but a brownish black. A suitable stain would be one made from black and vandyke brown. It may be mentioned here that black oak cannot be said to show up to the best advantage when finished out bright, the most satisfactory result being obtained by giving it a dull finish. The grain is frequently left unfilled.

Grain Imitation.—In matching, the wavy appearance of some woods may be given by a tremulous movement of the hand and by working the brush about in a varied manner, noting some adjacent portion of the wood as a guide to work from. It will also be noticed that most woods have a more or less mottled appearance, some showing the light and shade of the mottling much more prominently than others of the same class. It would be a mistake, therefore, to imitate some strongly marked mottling on a piece of wood which in itself presented very little of this kind of marking. The result would be out of keeping with the rest of the work.

Mottling may be imitated by working a rather broad, firm-bristled brush over the wet surface, lifting and pressing each corner alternately as the brush is worked from top to bottom. There is a knack in mottling, which the worker will, however, probably soon fall into. Veins may be put in with both a pencil and a tuft of wadding, the former for the finer veins, and the latter for the broader and firmer ones. Dip the pencil or wadding into the polish, then on to some dry colour of the required tint, and apply,

Staining and Polishing

taking some other part of the work as a pattern to go by.

A special rubber must be used for applying dyed polishes, and another rubber should be used to finish with clear polish. When finishing off, any trace of greasiness may be removed by well rubbing with a swab of clear rag, damped with spirits, on the face of which is spotted a few drops of glaze.

RE-POLISHING OLD FURNITURE.

The re-polishing of old furniture is akin to matching-up and improving, yet sufficiently distinct to merit treatment in a separate section. For some time there has been a growing tendency to re-cover and restore to their former position articles of furniture, etc., which, for many years, had only been found in lumber rooms and other out-of-the-way places. Many of the choicest specimens, which to-day realise high prices, have been picked up at country auction sales.

It should always be borne in mind that any article which was originally made correct to design cannot be improved upon, and that it is a mistake when restoring to add inlay where inlay was not intended, to carve the panels, etc., which were previously plain, or to add ornamental brass-work where it had been of a simple character, unless the restorer is thoroughly acquainted with the various styles. Above all, the colour of the wood should not, as a rule, be made darker.

The Aim of the Restorer should be to restore, as far as possible, everything as it was when first made, the only exception being that the colour should remain exactly as time had made it. One frequently sees very fine specimens of old oak panelling and carving completely spoilt by giving a coat of very dark stain, and then varnishing, when the proper course would have been to thoroughly clean, repair where faulty, match any new wood to the old, and oil or wax-polish. Any quantity of Chippendale work has had

Matching and Improving

inlay applied to the panels and legs, and turned ornaments added wherever possible, whereas inlay is never used in true Chippendale work. Then, who has not seen advertised—" Splendid carved oak grandfather clock " ? The case, without doubt, is old ; but the carving has been done very recently, for if you rub your hand over the carving the edges will almost cut your fingers, and the colour will be almost black. If the clock had been left alone, it would have been quite a plain oak case, with plain bold mouldings, and, except where dirt may have accumulated, the colour would be a dark brown.

REMOVING OLD POLISH.

In the best class of re-polishing it is necessary to remove the greater part of the old polish previous to applying the fresh, as new polish rarely takes nicely to the old. Where a perfect surface has to be dealt with, it is not advisable to scrape the work, as that would necessitate the use of a grain filler in order to fill up the pores of the wood ; while, if the polish is cleaned off by some other method, the old filling would not be removed, and the surface of the work would thus be left in a condition suitable for the immediate commencement of the application of the new polish. There are on the market a number of different preparations for removing old polish, and, although they may be a trifle expensive, their use saves a lot of time, and they can be recommended for efficiency.

Among the old-time methods of polish-removing, which it may be sometimes necessary to adopt, is that of saturating the surface of the work with methylated spirit in order to soften the lac. The work is well scoured with fine glass-paper, and the methylated spirit continually applied in order that the polish may not become lumpy under the glass-paper and so damage the surface of the wood. When all the polish has been softened, the work should be gone over with a piece of coarse rag saturated with spirit, in

Staining and Polishing

order to remove any remaining polish. A final rub over with No. 0 glass-paper leaves the work ready for polishing. If it is desired to remove but a part of the old polish, leaving the remainder in order to save time in bodying-in, the surface of the work should be gone over first with No. 1 and secondly with No. 0 glass-paper, using raw linseed oil as a lubricant on the face of the paper. When the work has been cut down sufficiently it can be gone over with a little methylated spirit on a piece of rag, in order to remove the superfluous oil, and the work will then be ready to receive its first coat of new polish.

REMOVING OLD VARNISH.

If it be desired to polish some old work, which has previously been varnished, the varnish must be removed. For this purpose there are many patent varnish removers, but as these are usually sold by the gallon (which will probably be more than the average reader will require), small quantities may be obtained from any painter, who always stocks these things for his own use. An old brush or a piece of rag should be used to put on the remover, which should be applied liberally, but kept on the surface of the article only, as it will damage anything it comes in contact with. Care should be taken to see that none of it gets on the clothes, or holes will quickly be burnt in by the destructive liquid. It will also burn the hands if allowed to stay on any time, and it will cause much pain, especially if it gets under the finger-nails. Two or three applications may be necessary, according to the quality and thickness of the varnished surface.

Ample time should be allowed for the liquid to soften up the gums, but no specified time can be given, as this depends upon the strength of the remover. This can be determined by a practical test. When sufficiently soft the varnish can be scraped off with a knife, a decorator's scraper being the best for flat surfaces. Commence at the

Matching and Improving

bottom of the article and work upwards, getting well into corners. If the varnish remover has been at all effective, the varnish should peel off readily as the knife touches it. Any mouldings or carved work are best cleaned out with shave-hooks, which can be had in various shapes. In Fig. 27 are illustrated two shapes, which will be found most convenient for this particular class of work. The head or blade may be ground to any desired shape, so as to fit any special hollow or projection. These tools are not pushed along

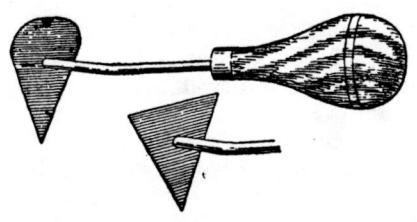

FIG. 27.—SHAVE-HOOKS.

like the scraper, but are dragged along. After all the varnish has been removed, and the work well cleaned off, it is the safest plan to wipe down with vinegar to kill any acid which may be left in the wood. Some firms, however, guarantee that no acid is used in their remover, and in these cases there is no need to use vinegar afterwards. Still, it is the safer plan to adopt.

A reliable Remover can be made by anyone by dissolving 1 part each of American potash or black ash, rock ammonia and soft soap, and 2 parts of common soda, in boiling water. The same instructions and advice as given above for patent removers apply also to this mixture. This must be followed by swilling down with clean water and then with vinegar. If care is not taken with this, however, the potash will darken the wood. When the work is dry, oil, fill in if necessary, and then polish. Sometimes an application of strong,

Staining and Polishing

hot soda solution will prove effective, and more so if some oxalic acid is added to it.

Spirit Varnish can usually be removed by simply washing with methylated spirit, which re-dissolves the lac. It is rather a long job by this method, but there is no fear of the wood being darkened by it, or of any subsequent action taking place.

RE-POLISHING.

Old Oak.—To restore very dirty old oak furniture it is best to thoroughly clean before repairing, which may be done by adding 1 lb. of American potash to 3 pints of boiling water, and apply it with a swab made by tying a piece of coarse rag round a stout stick or lath. Be careful not to put the hands in the mixture, or it will burn the skin off. After going over the work a few times, it will be soft enough to be scrubbed off. The scrubbing must be done with a fibre brush, as the potash mixture will make a hair brush soft. When all the dirt has been removed, the work must be allowed to get thoroughly dry, when it will be ready for repairing and cleaning up. Fine No. 2 glass-paper will be found the best for cleaning up old oak. Any new parts must be stained to match the old as far as possible.

The work can now be oiled and given a coat of yellow polish. When this is dry, paper with fine glass-paper, and shade where required by mixing a little vandyke brown with yellow polish and gas-black, if necessary, laid on with a camel-hair brush. The work may then be wax-polished, or given a few rubbers of yellow polish, tinted with a little vandyke brown. The brasswork, which should be removed before the woodwork is cleaned, should be placed in the hot potash for half-an-hour, and cleaned with a hard brush and ground emery or pumice stone, and then given a coat of light lacquer and placed in a warm oven for a few minutes. If the fittings are iron, they should be simply cleaned with the potash, and given a coat of Berlin black.

Matching and Improving

Very Old Oak which has been preserved from dust and dirt on the surface will be found to be of a rich brown colour, and as this is a natural colour great care should be taken that it is not spoilt in any way. In this case the article should be repaired first, and if it is possible to obtain old pieces of oak they would answer much better for repairing than new wood. When the repairing is finished, the surface should be oiled with linseed oil, and if by chance there should be any soiled parts the linseed oil will expose them. Should any be discovered, the parts should be scoured lightly with linseed oil and powdered pumice stone. The parts which have been repaired can be tinted to match the other wood by mixing raw umber, vandyke brown, or any other dry colour which will make a match, with yellow polish, and applied with a camel-hair brush. The whole of the work must now be rubbed over with a little turpentine (this is done to dry off the linseed oil), and then wax-polished. The polish used must not be very thick, and must be well rubbed in with clean dry cloths. This is a simple yet very efficient method to restore old woodwork, and articles treated in this manner will always attract the attention of good judges.

Cleaning Old Woodwork.—Furniture which had been in use for some time naturally becomes dirty, more especially in parts which dusters cannot reach properly, such as in corners of mouldings, carvings, etc. When, too, furniture cream has been used on the articles it works into quirks and corners, and, remaining partially soluble for a time, attracts dust and dirt, which, together with the furniture cream, has to be got rid of before re-polishing can be commenced by washing the work with warm water to which soda has been added in the proportion say, of a fair-sized handful of soda to half a gallon of water. With a moderately stiff brush, but one not stiff enough to damage the woodwork, scrub the old polish until clean, afterwards swilling the whole with cold water, but taking care not to use enough water to make any of the parts warp. Even

Staining and Polishing

if the bulk of the work has to be scraped previous to polishing, it is just as well to remove all the dirt by scouring, but it should be borne in mind that soda, if brought into direct contact with certain kinds of wood, has a tendency to darken their colour. After the old work has been washed any repairs necessary should be done previous to scraping.

WASHING FURNITURE.—Very few people know that furniture ought to be washed. One should take a bucket of tepid rain water and make a suds with a good pure soap. Then, with a soft piece of cheese-cloth, all the woodwork should be washed. It is astonishing how much dirt will come off. A second piece of cheese-cloth should be wrung dry out of hot water, and on this should be poured a teaspoonful of furniture polish or reviver. The heat will spread the polish through the cloth. Next, the furniture should be gone over with the second cloth. There will be no need of putting on more polish, for that much will do all one needs. Too many persons make the mistake of using too much polish and leaving it thick on the furniture, where it looks dauby and where it gathers more dirt. There is furniture in homes to-day that is cast off because of its appearance, when it might be brought back to its original freshness by this simple process of washing. Many persons do not know that a fine bit of mahogany is improved by careful washing, and hundreds of pianos have never been more than dusted in years. A square of cheese-cloth for the washing and another for the polishing will do the work.

REPAIRS.—In a handbook on Staining and Polishing the question of furniture repairing cannot be dealt with, although it is essentially an all-important part in restoration. Repairs, too, which are likely to be necessary can hardly be conjectured, as furniture repairers are required to set right every conceivable kind of damage. The most common faults are broken parts which either have to be supplied afresh or repaired, and the way the work has to be gone about depends upon the nature of the damage.

Matching and Improving

VENEERED WORK.

IN VENEERED WORK, for instance, one often finds that little pieces are broken off, or that blisters appear where the original glue failed to stick properly or has become soft by exposure to damp, etc. Where pieces of veneer are broken away fresh will have to be inserted, the jagged edges of the old being squared up in order to facilitate cutting a fresh piece to fit exactly the part to be covered. After the space has been cleared out to a reasonable shape, carefully cut out the old glue which is adhering to the wood with the assistance of a keen-edged chisel, but taking care not to cut the actual wood more than is absolutely necessary.

To fill up the hole a piece of veneer should be selected rather *thicker* than the original, which it should match in colour and figure as nearly as possible in order to save labour in matching-up stains.

BLISTERS of almost every conceivable size and shape are found in veneered work, and for setting these down there are a variety of different methods, each worker having his own way of dealing with them. A method which invariably works out satisfactorily is to cut away by means of a sharp-pointed knife the piece of veneer which has become unstuck, keeping the line of cutting as irregular as possible and avoiding sharp corners. After this the piece of veneer so loosened is removed bodily, the old glue carefully scraped off both veneer and groundwork, and the two re-glued and brought under pressure until dry. If the piece of blistered wood is very much swelled, it may be necessary to take a very fine shaving off in order to allow it to lie down flat again; but in doing this great care should be taken that too much is not pared away, as the swelling is certain to be very small and consequently very little of the veneer has to be removed. Small blisters may be pricked with a darning needle in two or three places, after which warm glue may be rubbed in with the finger tip and pressure applied.

Staining and Polishing

Another good method is to cut a nick in the blister with a thin penknife blade and insert a little glue under the blister.

Dents are nasty things to deal with, and if they are deep it is oftentimes better to let in a piece of veneer or thin wood than to attempt to raise them, while if they are shallow scraping the work will often take them out. However, if it is necessary that they be raised, the best plan to follow is to dissolve the polish on them with methylated spirit or one of the polish solvents which are obtainable from wholesale dealers in materials, and by repeated applications of hot water swell the wood to its original height.

Restoring the surface of the wood in this way generally necessitates scraping the whole surface of the piece so treated.

Scratches are usually best got out by scraping, although, if they are deep and the article is veneered with thin veneer, care should be taken that this is not scraped down too far. It will not be necessary in the case of narrow scratches to entirely remove them so long as the polish is scraped off the surface, as the process of filling in and polishing will help to disguise them.

Burns, if shallow, may be scraped away; but if deep, will require cutting out, a piece of similar wood being let in to level the surface up.

Pieces chipped off or out of woodwork, provided they are of any size, should be squared up and another piece of wood let in, while tiny holes may be filled up with wax.

Damaged Carved Portions can often have pieces of fresh wood let into them to take the place of the broken portions, which latter should of course be cleaned up square in order to admit of another piece of wood being fitted thereto, and the new piece being carved out to match the existing ornamentation.

DEFECTS IN POLISHING AND THEIR REMEDIES

Sweating — Cracks — Bruises— Blisters — Dulness— Finger-Marks—Fading—Scratches—Whiteness— Patchiness—Stains—Water-Marks—Salt-Marks

AS the beginner in French polishing may in his practice come across certain undesirable conditions which will need to be either cured entirely or at least improved in character, it will be necessary to deal with them here, though necessarily in a somewhat brief manner. There are many defects arising out of French polishing, some of which are due to bad workmanship, whilst others are caused by various other things. Sometimes the cause of failure may lie in the polish, while in other cases it may be caused by bad wood, poor tools, etc. A number of the evils which we here intend to deal with will be encountered on old polished work, which it is intended to re-polish; the rest may be experienced in the actual polishing process, either on new or old work.

SWEATING.

Sweating is perhaps the most common of all the defects to be found in French polished work, and is caused by the too liberal use of oil in the process of working. The oil ultimately breaks through the lac surface, and is noticeable by innumerable little fine lines. These lines become visible through the dust settling on the exuding oil. The sweating cannot be stopped entirely at once, as the oil will continue to force its way through on to the surface, and will probably take some months to cease. The disfigurement

Staining and Polishing

can, however, be mitigated to some extent by an occasional wipe over with a soft damp cloth.

The following is a good reviver: 3 ozs. paraffin, 3 ozs. vinegar, ½ oz. butter of antimony, and ½ oz. methylated spirit. This preparation should be applied to a swab of cotton wadding and used as an ordinary furniture cream, care being taken afterwards to rub the work clean with a dry soft duster.

As a reviver other workers use equal parts of lime water and raw linseed oil, with the addition of a small quantity of spirits. If the sweated portion has been allowed to stand for a considerable time and these revivers fail to clean it up, it will be necessary to remove all signs of the sweating by washing the surface with lukewarm water and monkey soap, or pumice-stone powder. When dry the work should be carefully glass-papered with No. 0 grade glass-paper and the work re-bodied up and spirited out.

Other causes of sweating are greasy wood-fillers, adulterated shellac, and a too liberal use of oil when oiling up the work so as to bring out the figure of the wood. Methylated spirit containing a large percentage of petroleum oil is another frequent cause of sweating.

Atmospheric moisture, owing to badly ventilated rooms, is often mistaken for actual sweating and it should immediately be removed with hot dusters and the work revived with a polish reviver. A little gum copal is often used in the polish to prevent sweating. Gum copal will not dissolve in methylated spirit; it is therefore usual to dissolve a little gum copal in 90 per cent. alcohol and add a little of this solution to the polish. Applying coat after coat of brush polish to the work and allowing insufficient time for each coat to set is another frequent cause of sweating.

CRACKS.

There are various causes of cracking. Sweating itself is often a cause of cracking, though the oil does not always

Defects in Polishing and their Remedies

break the lac surface to any considerable extent, such as would warrant us including it in this particular category. The evil which we are just now dealing with is much more apparent than simple sweating. It shows itself in the form of large and small fissures, extending over the work in various directions. A too common cause is the use of improperly seasoned wood to polish upon. The wood shrinks and swells, and causes the shellac film to break as a consequence. Cracking may also be due to the following causes:—

WHEN RE-POLISHING old work it is always advisable and very often necessary, to cleanse the work well by washing down with hot water and soda. If too much soda is used in the solution it will attack the old film of polish and cause it to perish. This means that the new surface is built upon a rotten foundation, which in turn will attack the upper coat of polish, the result being cracking, and often many other evils. Hence the need for care in washing down with a soda solution.

HARD POLISH.—Again, the old polish may be extremely hard—similar to that which is produced by the Continental system (see page 72)—and if a variety of polish which is of a much softer nature is applied on top, the result is almost certain to be a cracked surface. The uniting of a hard and softer film is a very prevalent cause of this evil. The result is, however, hastened or retarded according to the method adopted in beginning the re-polishing. If thick polish is in the first instance applied to the old surface, the trouble will soon show itself; but if, on the other hand, the work is wiped over with raw linseed oil after the cleaning of the old surface, then the result will not be so bad, as the oil helps the new polish to take more kindly to the old. If there is not perfect cohesion between the coats of polish the work is bound to be attended by serious evils. Therefore it is essential that the first few rubbers of polish should be used much diluted with spirit, the object being to soften up the old polish slightly, so that the new may adhere the more firmly to it.

Oil-Varnished Work.—It is also necessary here to caution the inexperienced reader against French polishing upon oil-varnished work of any description. In such a case the foundation is of so radically different a nature from French polish that the consequences cannot fail to be disastrous. The oil varnish is composed of oils and gums which readily respond to varying temperatures, and expand and contract according to the heat or cold to which they may be subjected. French polish is, on the other hand, of a more or less hard and brittle nature, and is not acted upon by different temperatures as oil varnish is. Consequently, the pulling of the elastic varnish in different directions underneath the French polish causes the latter to give away, and cracks are soon apparent.

Faulty Polish.—Using French polish that has been bought ready prepared may be another source of trouble, unless the spirit that was used in the polishing process was obtained from the same place as the polish. For instance, one needs spirit by itself, even if the polish has been bought ready made, as it will be necessary for use in the spiriting-out process, as well as at other times during the operation; and one brand of spirit may have been used in the preparation of the polish, and another brand used for diluting and clearing out.

Methylated Finish.—Or, again, what is called " methylated finish " may have been used instead of methylated spirits. This is made to avoid excise duty, and in one case is simply methylated spirits with a small quantity of naphtha added, while in another a small proportion of shellac or other gum is added to the spirit.

If the surface is very badly cracked, and will need re-polishing, cut down with powdered pumice stone and water, working in a circular direction so as to keep the whole surface even. If it is not cracked very badly, just cleanse

Defects in Polishing and their Remedies

the old surface by wiping over with a weak solution of water and common washing soda, applied hot. Wash down afterwards with clean cold water, and wipe thoroughly with a wash-leather. Then rub over with raw linseed oil, to freshen up the surface, and wipe off again, using clean rag. Now apply thin polish to the cracked surface, using plenty of spirit to enable the undercoat to soften up, thereby rendering it more easy for the new polish to amalgamate with it. Work each rubber out fairly dry before re-charging again, and spirit out instead of using glaze for the finish.

BRUISES.

Bruises may under certain conditions be taken out of furniture by damping the damaged portion and placing two thicknesses of good brown paper (or a few thicknesses of damp rag) on the bruised position. A hot iron poker is then held above the paper or rag; steam is thus generated and the damaged portion will swell up. It is then necessary to let the work dry for at least twenty-four hours; then paper it down, colour it up, and body up and finish in the usual manner. If this method fails to raise the timber (and this will be the case if the work has been splintered) nothing remains but to neatly insert a new piece of wood.

If, after raising a bruise, there is a body of polish on the surface, ordinary stains will not penetrate into the wood, and it will be necessary to resort to the method known as colouring-up or spirit staining. Spirit stains are made by dissolving spirit aniline dyes in methylated spirit or pure alcohol. These spirit stains may be applied to raw wood, and strike more deeply into the fibres than a water stain. Stains in nearly all cases may be applied warm, and to prevent undue raising of the grain the addition of a small quantity of glycerine may be advantageously used. Glycerine, however, is very slow in drying.

Staining and Polishing

BLISTERS.

A French-polished surface that has blistered can be renovated in the following manner: Wipe over the damaged portion with raw linseed oil, and then rub it well with fine glass-paper. This will remove the tops of the blisters, but may also remove some of the colour. In this latter case some suitable stain may be added to the polish, and thus the colour will be brought out fairly even. After rubbing down in the oil, re-polish as already described.

DULNESS.

When polish goes dull a day or so after it has been applied it may be safely concluded that there is either something wrong with the oil or with the way in which it has been applied. As we have stated before, linseed oil or poppy oil should be the only oils used, and then but sparingly. Dulness may be caused by not cleaning out the oil sufficiently when finishing off; or it may be caused by using the spirit rubber too wet when spiriting-out, thereby working up the under-coats and making the work patchy. If the surface is full of marks that will not clear out, it will be better to use the polish rubber again, using but the merest trace of oil. Then try spiriting out again.

FINGER-MARKS.

If, when but a few days old, a French-polished surface shows finger-marks when touched, it is clear evidence that it is of a greasy nature. This should not be the case, as good shellac and methylated spirits will yield a hard surface if properly applied. The defect betokens a too liberal use of oil or else the ingredients of the polish used were of a very soft character. The grease must be removed by wiping over with benzolene, or washing down the work, after which polish again, using "half-and-half," and be very sparing

Defects in Polishing and their Remedies

with the oil. Finish off in the usual manner and try the ox-gall treatment (see page 73).

FADING.

For restoring polish that has faded, either from damp, exposure to the sun, or other causes, it will be necessary to remove the upper surface of the polish, to colour the faded portion to match its surroundings, and to re-polish the whole. First of all cleanse down with a weak solution of soda and water, and if the surface is not very bad a good rubbing with spent glass-paper may be sufficient to remove all that is necessary. But if the surface is badly damaged and faded, sprinkle a few drops of methylated spirit on to the work and rub with No. 1 glass-paper. This will be sufficient to remove the upper surface only, and will also remove any dirt, furniture paste, or anything similar. A little powdered bath brick or pumice powder may be used to assist.

SCRATCHES.

If the scratches are but slight, they may be disguised somewhat by rubbing with raw linseed oil. But if the scratches are deep, then the polish will need to be removed to get down to the level (or nearly so) of the bottom of the deepest scratches. The portions that are damaged must be scraped and glass-papered off, though sometimes it is possible to draw them up level by pressing a fairly hot iron against a wet rag which is laid over the defective parts. In any case re-polishing will be necessary. If the polish is simply removed from the damaged parts, such parts will be lighter in colour, and besides having to be matched up will need to be brought up to the same level as the surrounding polish, which is a difficult task. Hence the better plan is to remove all the polish from the article, or that side of the article which happens to be damaged, and then re-polish in the ordinary way.

Staining and Polishing

WHITENESS.

The Whitening (or showing white marks) of a French-polished surface may be due to any of the under-mentioned causes. When benzolene or anything of a similarly hot nature has been used in the filling-up of the grain, either in conjunction with plaster, whiting, or any other filling material, it causes the polish to show white in the grain. A similar result will be obtained by omitting to use vinegar over work which has just been bleached with oxalic acid. Sometimes plaster-of-paris contains lime, and when such is used as a filler the lime will eat off the stain and show up the whiteness of the wood in that particular part. Or again, perhaps the wood has been merely surface-stained, and the stain has got rubbed off the edges and sharp members of mouldings in working up the polish. The stain should be allowed to work well into the wood, and thus avert the danger of being so easily rubbed off.

White Streaks may be caused by applying polish before water stains have become thoroughly dry; or by using spirits adulterated with benzolene; or by cleaning up veneer before the glue has thoroughly dried; or by excessive damp acting on the polish in some manner or other. The colour may sometimes be restored by wiping over with raw linseed oil and turpentine in equal quantities, and afterwards cleaning out with spirits. In many cases, however, nothing short of re-polishing will prove effective as a cure. Excessive moisture is a frequent cause of polished work turning white. The moisture may be present owing to the work not having been wiped quite dry after washing, or it may be in the materials in some way or other. To remedy it remove the work, if at all possible, to a warm room, and rub very briskly with a piece of flannel made fairly damp with spirits and linseed oil in equal proportions. Next give it a good rubber of polish, and then a good flowing coat of newly-made spirit varnish. The warmth of the room and the new polish and varnish

Defects in Polishing and their Remedies

combined should prove effective in restoring the colour. The work may be enriched in colour by adding a little stain either in the polish or the varnish.

PATCHINESS.

Dark Patches may be removed by repeated applications of oxalic acid in water. Swill off with clean water, and finally wipe over with common vinegar to neutralise any trace of the acid. This treatment, especially if the oxalic acid solution is used too strong, may remove the polish also. If this does take place, wipe over with raw linseed oil after the acid has been washed off, neutralised, and the work is thoroughly dry. Then re-polish, or bring up the surface with beeswax and turpentine. If the dark patch is caused by paraffin—such as may happen by a paraffin lamp having stood on the polished surface—it may be removed by rubbing with benzolene. But if this is not sufficiently effective, the use of oxalic acid, as just described, must be resorted to. If there is a light patch, which has probably been caused by water or damp, try rubbing with paraffin. This is generally effective.

STAINS.

Ink and Other Stains may be removed by the same process as we have described for removing dark patches—namely, the oxalic acid process. Where the stains are particularly obstinate a piece of rag saturated with a strong solution of acid and water may be left on the wood until the discoloration has gone; and, if it is necessary, the rag may be re-charged with the acid and again applied to the work. Of course this will destroy the polish, and to a certain extent will bleach the wood underneath. It will then require colouring-up with chemical stains to match its surroundings before re-polishing.

Staining and Polishing

WATER-MARKS.

These are caused by water falling on the polished surface and being allowed to stay there for some time. The water will leave a mark much more readily on a French-polished surface than on an oil-varnished surface. Polishes containing an excess of soft gums or of resin are most susceptible to these influences. The original colour can often be restored by wiping the work over with linseed oil, and then rubbing the surface with a swab of clean rag made moist with methylated spirits. It should be applied lightly at first, but as the spirit dries out of the rubber more pressure should be employed. When the surface has been restored to its original colour, and all traces of greasiness are removed wipe over with benzolene; or else wipe over with a solution of common washing soda, using a lump of soda about the size of a walnut to 1 pint of water. Afterwards give the work, if it be other than furniture, an even-flowing coat of a good quality of copal varnish. This will produce a better wearing surface than anything else, and will not readily mark with water.

Marks on furniture made by hot jugs or plates left standing on the polished surface will have to be rubbed down and re-polished in the usual manner.

SALT-MARKS.

Everyone knows that at any seaside place there are what might be termed salt particles in the atmosphere. This saltness is detrimental to French-polished work, eating into the polish and destroying its nature. To avoid this, great pains must be taken in the polishing process so as to get a good body of polish on to the work. When starting with the new work apply three or four coats of thin polish, either with a pad or a camel-hair brush. Now rub down quite smooth and even with pumice powder and linseed oil, using a piece of felt for the purpose. Wipe down

Defects in Polishing and their Remedies

perfectly clean after this operation, and then finish with a waterproof polish made as follows: Take 3 ozs. of gum benzoin, 1 oz. of gum sandarac, 1 oz. of gum-animi, and dissolve the lot in 1 pint of methylated spirits. Strain off, and add ¼ gill of poppy oil.

EXAMPLE OF INLAY WORK.

Another method is to body up as if for spiriting-out in a proper manner; but, when the spiriting-out stage is reached, dull the work down with pumice-stone powder and water to kill any trace of oil, and then finish off with one or more coats of a good quality of outside oil varnish. This is for new work. For old work, cleanse with a weak solution of soda and water, and re-polish to gain a good colour. Kill the oil by wiping over with benzolene, and finally apply a flowing coat of oil varnish made specially for outside work. It may be well to add that, although French polishing must not on any account take place on an oil-varnish surface, it is quite safe to put an oil varnish upon an ordinary French-polished surface.

Staining and Polishing

INLAID PANEL—JAPANESE.

POLISHING INLAID WORK, Etc.

Inlaid Work—Marquetry Transfers—Polishing Turned Work—Polishing Fretwork

IN dealing with the polishing of inlaid work it must be clearly understood that no one process can be given that will cover the whole ground of inlaying. The use of different woods in the different designs necessitates different methods of working. For instance, a design which did not include any white woods could be polished with ordinary brown polish made from orange shellac; but if white or very light woods, such as holly, boxwood, or satinwood, formed part of the design, then we should have to use either a white or transparent polish, so as not to destroy the whiteness of these woods.

Then there is the question of fillers. If a paste filler is used it will readily be seen that we cannot use the same for very dark woods or a black-stained wood as we use for light woods. But for such woods as are not of a particularly open grain other methods of filling can be employed, as we shall show in the course of this chapter. Then, again, some of the woods may need lightening, others may need darkening a little, while in some cases full staining may have to be resorted to. All these varying circumstances call for different methods of treatment.

Inlaid Box.—The application of marquetry and intarsia is usually restricted to workboxes, picture-frames, fancy trays, and to any kind of fancy articles. We will, however, commence by taking a typical example of modern marquetry work, as illustrated in Fig. 28.

We will suppose that this design is ornamenting a walnut workbox which is newly made and has no kind of preparation whatever. The design is composed of very thin veneers of various colours, such as black, art green, rose pink, mauve, pale gold and purple. We cannot of course

Staining and Polishing

represent all these colours in the drawing, neither does it matter, for this class of work is executed in all colours. It is sufficient for our purpose to note that both light and dark

FIG. 28.—AN INLAID WORKBOX LID, SHOWING PORTION OF BORDER AND PART OF CENTRE PLATE.

coloured woods are used; and thus we shall have to use a polish which will not impair the tone of any of the colours.

Fortunately no fillers are required for these veneers, so that all we shall need to trouble about in this connection will be the walnut surrounding the design. This portion of the box will need to be brought up in the manner described in previous chapters. After all has been well

Polishing Inlaid Work, etc.

glass-papered, and all bits of glue removed from the surface, the walnut should be oiled to bring out the figure and beauty of the wood. If any staining is required to alter or darken the natural colour of the walnut, this may be done by carefully cutting round the design by the aid of a small brush with the stain desired.

If the walnut needs to be filled, make a filler of methylated spirits and whiting, or turpentine and whiting, with a little pumice powder added, and tint with vandyke brown to get the walnut shade. This will be difficult to apply without entrenching on the marquetry work, so that it will be necessary to protect the latter. For this purpose coat the edges of the inlay work with heavy polish and allow it to dry hard before filling. When the latter operation is finished, and the filling is set, the polish may be washed off with methylated spirits. After cleaning all up again, proceed with the polishing as directed in previous chapters. The polish, however, must be a transparent one, so that the whole of the box can be polished at the same time. In marquetry work always use white or transparent polish.

Inlaid Table.—We will now take a mahogany table which is inlaid with satinwood and a green-stained wood, after the style of Sheraton furniture. The table has, however, been stained walnut colour previously, and it is now desired to have it altered, the walnut polish to be removed, and the table to be polished up in its natural colour—mahogany. The walnut polish must first be removed by using a scraper, care being taken to see that the surface of the wood is not cut or abraded by the action of the scraper. After all has been carefully removed, clean up and oil with red oil. If the colour of the wood needs brightening up, use a red stain, composed of bismarck brown dissolved in equal parts of polish and spirits. In staining, the inlay must be protected by coating with brush polish applied with a pencil brush. If, however, the polisher thinks he can safely cut round the inlay with the stain he may do so, in which case the coating with brush polish would be unneces-

Staining and Polishing

sary. Still it is advisable, as if a paste filler is to be used as well the protective coating of the inlay will do for both the staining and filling operations. After both these processes the stain and filler which have covered the inlay can be wiped off quite clean and the polishing proceeded with.

If the surface has had polish applied previous to the staining, water stains will be useless for the latter purpose; hence spirit stains must be used. It may be that the scraping off of the walnut polish has not disturbed the old filling. In this case it will not be necessary to fill up again properly; but a couple of coats of spirit varnish will be useful in obtaining a smooth level surface. When it is dry and hard, rub down with pumice powder and raw linseed oil, using a piece of felt for the purpose. Should a paste filler be needed, mix dry Venetian red instead of vandyke brown. Another method is to totally ignore the inlay until the spiriting-out stage is reached, the work being filled up, and brought up with coloured polish over the entire surface; when well bodied up and ready for the final stage, the polish, etc., over the inlay is scraped off with a sharp narrow scraper or knife. This method, however, does not leave a perfectly level surface on the work and should if possible be avoided. The inlay then receives two or three coats of clear spirit varnish, and when brought up well above the surrounding surface the whole is ground down to one level with pumice powder, and afterwards spirited out.

Intarsia.—Having dealt with the form of inlaying known as marquetry, and with ordinary inlay banding and centres so common on general furniture, we will now select for treatment a form of inlay work known as intarsia. This is generally of a simple design in which pictorial effect is obtained by a few pieces of inlay, the grain and outlay of which represents a land or seascape without detail. A sketch of a simple yet effective design for this class of work is shown in Fig. 29. Six woods are recommended for the making of this picture—maple, light oak, satin walnut, dark walnut, padouk and white chestnut. We will therefore suppose

Polishing Inlaid Work, etc.

that this inlay picture has been made according to instructions given, and is now ready for the finishing treatment, which has to be done in a first-class manner.

Assuming that all the woods have been papered down to one smooth level and well dusted, we must first consider the nature of the woods which have been selected. Some will be very open-grained, whilst others are close and fine in texture; and in addition there is the porosity of the

FIG. 29.—A PICTORIAL INLAY.

woods to take into consideration, some being more absorbent than others. Light oak is very coarse and open, and padouk (although a very hard and close-grained wood taken on the whole) possesses innumerable small fissures which require filling up. Dark walnut is another of the woods which require a filler. The other three are sufficiently close-grained to warrant our dispensing with an ordinary filler such as we propose to use on the above-named woods.

Filler.—Some reader might think it unnecessary to use a filler at all when dealing with work of this character, but, if we are to polish it as we have proposed, the polish will make the grain stand out much more prominently than it does when in its natural state, and consequently the different textures of the woods—some close and solid,

Staining and Polishing

with others open and apparently unfinished—will give an appearance entirely unsatisfactory.

Grain.—One reservation we must make, however, and it is this: that, where the grain of the wood is chosen to represent something in the picture, it should certainly be left as much as possible in its original state, so as to express itself as fully as possible. For instance, any wood which possesses a decidedly wavy grain will be eminently suitable for representing the waves in a seascape. And again, if a design is to be worked which is representative of fruit or natural foliage, and which contains berries, what more adapted for this purpose than the "eyes" of bird's-eye maple, or a choice bit of burr walnut? In such cases as these, where each piece of wood is specially chosen to represent each part of the design because of the similarity of the grain or the colour of the wood to the form or colour of the object imitated, it is certainly the better plan to do nothing as regards either staining or filling, but simply to polish it over as neatly as possible with transparent polish. That is the ideal way to do such work, but it is not always practicable, and it happens that in the example which we have chosen the method is unsuitable. The light oak, the dark walnut and the padouk each requires a filler, but, owing to the colours being so markedly different, a white filler would not be right, nor would any filler which might be made suitable for one of the woods be suitable for either of the other two.

The Filler could be made from turpentine and whiting, or methylated spirits and whiting, tinted to the shade required for each of these woods. The oak would require a yellowish filler, the dark walnut a brownish filler, and the padouk a red filler. For the first-named add a little ochre or raw sienna to the filler; for the next one add instead vandyke brown, while for padouk add Venetian red. As these coloured fillers would stain the white woods if put on them, it must be seen that none of the filler is allowed to trespass on those woods. This will be found

Polishing Inlaid Work, etc.

a difficult matter, unless precaution is taken to protect them. This may be accomplished by varnishing with spirit varnish on those parts immediately touching the portions to be filled. After the filling is complete the spirit varnish may be washed off with methylated spirits; or, better still, it may be rubbed down with glass-paper.

Staining.—If it be desired to stain or darken some of the woods employed, it should be done for preference before any polishing is done, when any kind of stain may be used. Should it be necessary to stain a little after the application of polish, spirit stains should be used, but no coloured polish can be used to bring up the tone of any of the woods, owing to the presence of white woods in the design. Where two or more woods which possess little difference in colour are placed against each other, staining may be resorted to to give distinction to them. What is meant here, however, is simply darkening one and bleaching another, and not the application of vivid colouring which might spoil the whole scheme. Some distinction may also be given to similarly toned sections which happen to be close to each other by rubbing black wax or shoemaker's heelball in all the joinings of the several pieces.

In Polishing the picture it will be noticed that some sections absorb considerably more polish than do others, and it will therefore be necessary to give the more absorbent woods an extra coat or two of polish, applied with the brush, so as to bring them up to the others. Whilst bodying-up, a little pumice powder must be dabbed on to the work at intervals and worked into the wood with the polish. This will fill up evenly all parts of the work, and will present a good, solid surface for spiriting-out.

MARQUETRY TRANSFERS.

Sheraton furniture being very popular, a few hints on the application and polishing of marquetry transfers may be given here.

Staining and Polishing

At the present time imitations of bandings, stringings, painted decoration and marquetry work in many styles (not only Sheraton) can be bought in the form of transfers. These are used for various purposes, from lettering tramcars and railway carriages to decorating furniture and iron mantelpieces.

A Transfer is a very thin film, in natural wood or veneer colours, mounted face downwards on paper or celluloid. When duly transferred to the wood it is a wonderfully true representation of inlay work, and the method of laying is fairly simple.

The wood should be bodied up and finished in the usual way and allowed to thoroughly harden. It should then be slightly rubbed down with a little powdered pumice stone in the direction of the grain. The transfer (which should have all unnecessary paper removed from it by carefully cutting it out, similar to "scraps" on the old-fashioned draught screens) is dipped in a solution of gelatine and water ($\frac{1}{2}$ oz. of gelatine to 1 pint of water is the correct proportion) and pressed well down on the polished surface, care being taken to work out any air bubbles. Leave the transfer to thoroughly dry and then take a damp sponge and saturate the back. After the water has soaked through the paper, gently lift one corner and gradually *lift* the entire paper away. Do not attempt to *slide* the paper off or failure will result.

Carefully wipe away any slimy matter around the transfer and leave it to dry. When the transfer is set it can be fastened by applying at intervals two coats of thin white polish, which should be applied with a camel-hair mop brush in a similar manner to fastening after colouring-up. When dry, finish with the rubber in the ordinary way.

Some polishers prefer to use methylated spirits in which to dip the transfer, but great care is required, as the spirit is liable to re-dissolve the shellac body on the polished work. The methylated spirit method answers well for small surfaces, such as transferring the maker's name to

Polishing Inlaid Work, etc.

a piano, etc., but it should only be used by men experienced in the work.

POLISHING TURNED WORK.

These instructions would not be complete without some reference to the polishing of turned work in the lathe. Such things as tool-handles, knobs, small pillars, spindles, etc., are most conveniently polished in the lathe. The larger class of turned work, such as newel posts, table-legs, etc., are best treated by hand—that is, polished in the ordinary way without the aid of machinery. They could, however, be polished in the lathe if it be specially desired. For this kind of polishing the hard woods cause less trouble than the soft woods and give better results. Especially is this the case if the latter are stained, and if water stains are used. These, as we have before observed, have a tendency to raise the grain, and they are a source of much trouble to the polisher in his endeavour to obtain a smooth surface. Tact and skill would then be called into requisition, and the novice is therefore advised to adopt a safer plan and to use either an oil or spirit stain, both of which are much less liable to raise the grain of the wood than is a water stain. Also a spirit stain may be added to the polish, which is a further advantage.

In Preparing for the staining and polishing it should be seen that the articles are turned quite smooth and that they are free from any machine oil. The latter is not a drying oil, and is bound to damage the work. Glass-paper should be used very sparingly, as there is a danger of rounding off what should be sharp angular members. A much better plan is to use some of the shavings of the wood, pressing them against the article as it revolves. It may not be out of place to mention here that a passable finish can be gained on hard wood articles by simply oiling, and then polishing off by holding shavings against them. If working upon soft wood articles that are not required to be stained,

Staining and Polishing

they should first be coated with either brush polish or spirit varnish, and then oiled and smoothed off with the shavings. Now comes the question of filling-in. Hard, close-grained woods, of course, rarely if ever require the use of grain-fillers. But if the wood be such that a filler is required, the article should be wiped over with a little boiled linseed oil, and the filler (made from dry whiting tinted to the colour of the wood) rubbed into the work as it revolves somewhat slowly. The grain will get filled and the surface cleaned at the same time.

The Rubber for polishing should simply be a tuft of wadding without the rag covering, as it is easier to work well into the hollows and quirks. It is better if the wadding has been previously used, so that there is no danger of any loose cotton becoming detached whilst polishing. To charge, pour the polish on to the rubber and break it up a little to distribute the polish. In making the latter it will be noticed that it differs somewhat from the ordinary French polish. To make it, dissolve 1 oz. of the best quality of beeswax in sufficient turpentine to make a thin paste. Obtain another jar, and in it place ½ pint of methylated spirits, 1 oz. of gum benzoin, 1 oz. gum sandarac, and 1 oz. of seed lac or best quality button lac. Dissolve the lot by gentle heat, and when sufficiently liquefied and well mixed strain through a piece of fine muslin. Then mix it thoroughly with the wax and turpentine. The same kind of polish is used for both hard and soft woods.

In applying the Polish the article should be revolved, but slowly at first, and care must be taken to see that the wadding rubber does not adhere to any portion of the work. After using the contents of the first rubber, oil the work rather sparingly, and then hold a handful of the shavings left from turning firmly against it, which will level the work and thus secure a smooth surface for future operations. When it comes to the spiriting stage the lathe should be run at a high speed, and instead of using the

Polishing Inlaid Work, etc.

wadding rubber a soft piece of chamois leather should be damped with spirits and applied to the article very softly at first, more pressure being applied as the spirits work out.

Methods of supporting turned work when polishing by hand have been given on page 74.

POLISHING FRETWORK.

When staining and polishing fretwork is attempted the work should be taken to pieces and mounted in a

FIG. 30.—WAD RUBBER FOR POLISHING FRETWORK.

somewhat similar manner to one of the methods shown on page 75.

Spirit stains are preferred to water stains, as the latter, owing to their slower drying qualities, are liable to twist and warp the wood.

If the fretwork be in an open-grained wood it will require to be filled in by using a suitably coloured filler which can be applied with a brush. Oil the work with red or ordinary linseed oil as may be thought necessary, and proceed to polish in the usual manner. Prepare a wad-rubber as shown at Fig. 30, which may be made by cutting a strip of closely woven woollen cloth about $1\frac{1}{4}$ ins. wide and rolled up as shown in the illustration.

Staining and Polishing

This wad-rubber may be tacked together with a needle and thread on its top face, or held in position by slipping an elastic band over it as shown in the sketch. The rubber is charged with polish in the usual manner and two thicknesses of rag covering placed over its face ; the ends of the rag are then gathered up similar to those of the pounce bag shown on page 48, and the wad-rubber is ready for use.

Another temporary method of making a wad-rubber for fretwork polishing is to insert a large, flat-faced bone button in two or three thicknesses of white wadding which have previously been saturated with polish, and draw up the ends of the wadding and covering rag, similar to the pounce bag. The advantage of this type of rubber is that it gives a flatter surface to the work and does not catch and tear up so easily as the polishing rubber shown on page 123. It also gives a more even distribution of polish to the fretted surface.

The Method of Bodying-up, etc., is exactly the same as already described, except that the internal edges of the fretwork are proceeded with first. Then polish the back of the work, and lastly the face ; any tears of polish which have run out on to the face of the work when polishing the edges can thus be removed with glass-paper, and a level surface left on the back and face before the finishing stage is reached.

For First-class Work, such as grand piano music rests, the internal edges of the frets are more or less rub-polished. This is done by saturating a strip of fine rag with polish and wrapping it around a round wooden skewer or other suitably shaped piece of wood, such as a square wooden skewer of about $\frac{1}{4}$-in. sides. The rubber so made can be easily threaded through the frets, but of course a great amount of time has to be expended on the work.

For ordinary frets the polish or spirit varnish is applied to the internal edges with a pencil brush.

OAK AND ITS VARIOUS FINISHES

Fuming—Dark and Antique Oak—Green and Grey Oak—Polishing Oak Coffins—Bleached Oak

A S oak is one of the most popular woods in furniture making, and as its surface is capable of many varied and attractive treatments, some of these may be dealt with specifically here.

FUMING OR FUMIGATING.

Fuming, or Fumigating, means the exposure of wood to the fumes of ammonia, and one of the favourite methods of finishing oak is to fumigate it and afterwards finish with wax-polishing. An idea of what ammonia fumes will do in this direction may be gathered by holding a small piece of clean, new oak tightly over the neck of an uncorked bottle of the liquid. In five minutes the wood will have toned down considerably. Two incidental advantages of fuming are that the process does not raise the grain and that the colour procured is not readily liable to fade.

Oak may of course be darkened by giving it repeated coats of diluted ammonia. This is a simple staining method, but the fuming process requires some explanation. Care should be taken when using ammonia, as the fumes, when inhaled, are dangerous.

When buying ammonia for fumigating, ask for "point eight eighty," this being full strength (specific gravity ·880). For the actual work no particular skill is needed, and the following method is easy of manipulation. See that the article to be treated is free from dust and greasy fingermarks, and that drawer and cupboard doors are left open; if any portion be not freely exposed to the action of the fume it will not be darkened.

A large cupboard or box (or a small room if the article is large) that is fairly airtight will answer as a fumigating

Staining and Polishing

chamber, the work being left exposed to the fume of the ammonia solution from four to twelve hours, according to the colour required and the quality of the oak used. A well-made packing case, with strong brown paper pasted over the joints, will do.

The Liquid Ammonia is placed on the floor or (as convenient) in shallow dishes, so arranged that the fumes will come well around the work. Seal all cracks, holes and other openings to prevent the escape of fumes. In order, however, to ascertain the progress of the work, it is well to leave a stick (tight-fitting) pushed through a hole in the side of the box; this can be drawn out at certain intervals to see how the work is progressing. It is essential that the stick used be of the same kind of wood as the object being fumigated, otherwise the correct state of the article cannot be gauged. Another good plan is to have a pane of glass in the side of the box, through which the progress of the work can be watched.

If it is found that certain parts of a piece of work are dark enough, and that others are still light in colour, give the dark portions two coats of white polish or wax and again fume the work so as to tone the light portions down. A second fumigating of articles that have been treated with two coats of polish will have no effect on them. After taking the work from the fume leave it in the air for a few hours to sweeten, after which oil it if thought necessary and give it two coats of white polish with a camel-hair mop brush. When dry and hard, glass-paper it down quite smooth, and then wax-polish or French polish if desired.

It occasionally happens that, when an article of furniture is composed of oak from different logs (especially in the case of chair frames which are generally made up from various cuttings of oak), in the fumigation process there is a discrepancy of colour, one portion taking the fume darker than the other, or taking it a little darker than is required to match existing work. The dark portion may be bleached to a certain extent by dissolving oxalic acid

Oak and its Various Finishes

in methylated spirit, and applying it warm to the dark portions by painting it on with an old camel-hair mop brush. The solution is highly poisonous, and it is advisable for this reason to keep it off one's fingers. When the bleached parts have been neutralised with vinegar, the work when dry should be glass-papered down.

Fumigated oak is usually finished by wax-polishing, described on page 137.

VARIOUS STAINED OAKS.

Dark Oak.—Another method of darkening oak—say, the wood of an existing piece of furniture—is as follows: Wash down with lukewarm water, Brook's soap, and a little finely-powdered bath brick. Let the work thoroughly dry, and paper the grain down with No. 1 or No. 0 glass-paper. Take one part of French polish and two parts of methylated spirit and mix them together. Take vandyke brown $\frac{1}{4}$ oz. and vegetable-black as much as will lie on a shilling; put these in the powdered form into a piece of fine old cambric, and tie up the corners so as to form a bag. Dip the bag containing the dry powder bodily into the thinned polish, and squeeze through your fingers so as to extract the colour until the polish is of the required tint. Do not make the polish too dark. It is better to give two applications to the work than to make the polish too dark at first. When the coloured polish is the required shade apply quickly in the direction of the grain with a camel-hair mop brush. Let the polish dry for a couple of hours. Then give the work a coat of pure polish, which will have the effect of fastening the colour, and proceed to finish in the usual manner by use of the rubber or by wax-polishing.

Oak may be slowly darkened by coating with a 2 per cent. solution of bichromate of potash to which has been added $\frac{1}{2}$ per cent. of dilute nitric acid. The tone gained is particularly rich and warm, but the process takes a long

Staining and Polishing

time—usually a few weeks, or a little more, to get a really good colour. The figure and veining of the wood can be brought into strong relief by treating first with a weak decoction of brown madder, and, when this is dry, painting with a solution of acetate of lead.

Antique Oak.—The " antique " effect on oak is usually obtained on straight-grain timber. The filler used is darkened with burnt umber or vandyke brown (or a mixture of both), or with drop black and burnt umber. For a very dark effect the wood may be stained before filling. In this case make up a stain of 2 parts vandyke brown, 1 part raw umber, and ½ part drop black, all ground in oil. Mix this with brown japan, thinning for use with turpentine.

Oak may also be given an antique colour by applying several coats of ammonia diluted in water; or a quick method is to make a stain of iron filings and vinegar or a concentrated solution of permanganate of potash.

Cathedral Oak is another term for a dark brown stained oak. Make a stain by mixing 1 oz. permanganate of potash in 1 quart of water (or proportionately), and give the wood two coats. Let the first coat dry and lightly glass-paper before applying the second. Glass-paper again and give a coat of ebony filler (see page 56). Wipe off, let the work stand overnight, glass-paper, and give a coat of white shellac. Finally, glass-paper again and wax-polish the surface to a flat finish—that is, without rubbing up the wax.

The Flemish Oak finish, with its rich coffee colour, is usually done on quarter-sawn oak. A stain made up in the proportion of ¼ lb. bichromate of potash and ½ gallon of water is strained and applied with a bristle brush. When dry, glass-paper with No. o paper, then mix up some japan drop black with turpentine, and give the work one coat of this stain. Wipe off clean, then apply a coat of orange shellac. Let the work stand a few hours, then smooth up

Oak and its Various Finishes

with fine paper. Another coat of shellac may be given, and, when hard, rub with pumice-stone powder and oil to a surface. The colour shows up in the pores very dark. The wood should not be finished with a lustre, nor should the pores be perfectly filled.

Mission Oak.—The effect obtained on the well-known American "Mission" style of furniture is something of a dead black relieved by a suspicion of grey. A stain can be made from 1 lb. drop black in oil, ½ oz. of rose pink in oil, thinned with one gill of good japan drier and 1½ pints of turpentine. Strain through doubled cheese-cloth. Japan colours may be used in place of oil colours, but in this case omit the driers and add a little rubbing varnish to bind the stain. Finish as usual with wax.

Green Oak.—Certain grades of Russian and Austrian oak, when fumigated by ammonia, naturally assume the peculiar greenish tint which is so much admired. If, after fumigation, any portions are too light in colour, they are coloured up by dissolving suitable pigments in methylated spirits. If the article engaged upon is made of the open-grained American oak, fumigation will have little or no effect upon it, and it may be lightly stained with, say, Stephens' or Johnson's fumed oak stain, which will give it a greenish tinge. To colour up the work, obtain a little aniline green in powder and strain white polish through this dye. This will give a green that will be of a very brilliant hue, and it will have to be darkened by the addition of a little spirit black and spirit blue. The spirit blue can be made by dissolving the ordinary Reckitts' blue in methylated spirits. If the work is to be filled in, so as to choke up the pores, a little of the colour should be added to the filler. Remember that aniline green is treacherous and a few grains will colour a pint of spirits.

Another green stain is obtainable by mixing together ½ lb. chrome green and ¼ lb. chrome yellow, both of medium shade. In another vessel mix together 1½ pints of turpentine,

Staining and Polishing

½ pint of raw linseed oil, and a little good white japan. Thin the colour mixture with this, and apply one coat. When dry, apply a coat of white shellac, coloured just a little with turmeric and a few grains of green aniline. Give a wax finish.

There is also a rather uncommon style of finishing oak, known as "verde" green. The effect is obtained by staining the wood with a not over-strong black dye, and using a bright green wood grain-filler. When this is dry the work is coated all over with asphaltum dissolved in coal-tar naphtha, and as the stain does not penetrate those parts protected with varnish the result is unique. The varnish used, though of a rather quick-drying nature, differs from our spirit varnish, as it contains practically no shellac, the nearest approach to it being what is sometimes called French oil-varnish. For dulling purposes specially made brushes are used, these being soaked in oil and dipped occasionally into fine-grade pumice-stone powder and brushed well over the varnished surface. This treatment, when the surface has thoroughly hardened, soon removes its brightness without scratching it, any excess of oil being afterwards removed with plenty of clean rag.

Silver Grey Oak.—The oxidised silver effect seen on oak furniture can be obtained in the following way: Smooth with No. 0 glass-paper, then stain with a preparation of ½ part silver nitrate and 20 to 25 parts water (both by weight). Apply two coats of this, then a coat of commercial hydrochloric acid. When dry, apply a coat of ammonia water of ordinary strength. If the work can be left to dry in the dark it will give a still better effect. The finish may be in oil or varnish, but in any case it must not be bright. An eggshell or mat surface is what is required. This stain may also be used on woods such as poplar, birch, beech and pine.

Polishing Oak Coffins.—Oak and elm coffins may be polished in the following manner: First wipe over with

Oak and its Various Finishes

linseed oil, and then fill the grain up with a filler made from whiting and turpentine, mixed fairly stiff. Stain the filler with dry colours to match the colour of the wood; for oak use ochre, and for elm use ochre and Venetian red. Make a rubber fairly large, and with a good supply of French polish give the work a wipe over. Repeat this operation two or three times until a fair body is got on the coffin. Smooth down with very fine glass-paper and give a coat of naphtha varnish. When this is dry, smooth the surface down with another rubber of polish, gradually thinning out with spirit. Next apply another coat of varnish, when the work may be considered completed. If the job will allow, the lid may be finished off better by giving it another rub over with the polish to smooth the varnish down, then finishing off with glaze, or spiriting-out properly. Wood naphtha should be used as a solvent for the polish and varnish rather than methylated spirits. This method gives a fairly good finish; but for a very cheap job, some only give the coffins a good wipe over with linseed oil, or a coat or two of a quick-drying varnish. Very often the plinth and moulding on elm coffins are finished to represent mahogany. This is done by coating with red polish.

The method used for supporting coffins whilst polishing them is similar to that used to support a drawer (page 74).

Oak coffins are in some cases fumigated, oiled and wax-polished; or fumigated, oiled and finished by the spirit-varnish method.

For Re-polishing Old Oak, see pages 96 and 97.

BLEACHED OAK.

Light or Bleached Oak work is used for show cases and window fitments of jewellers' shops, etc., the timber used being Indiana white quartered oak. If prime wood can be obtained it should be filled in as follows: In ½ gallon of tepid water dissolve 1 oz. of alum, and add dry powdered

Staining and Polishing

whiting to bring it to the consistency of a paste filler, When effervescing has ceased, add a very small quantity of yellow ochre and a little ground size to form a binder. Fill in the work and bring up to a finish with white polish. On no account oil the work after filling.

STATIONERY CABINET WITH MARQUETRY INLAY TRANSFER (see page 119).

If prime timber cannot be procured, use a good light-coloured oak and bleach it up with oxalic acid solution.

About two hours after the acid solution has dried, neutralise by washing the work down with vinegar; when the work is thoroughly dry fill in and polish. The oxalic acid solution is made by dissolving $1\frac{1}{2}$ oz. of oxalic acid in 1 pint of hot water; it should be applied with a piece of clean rag which should be tied to a stick so as to form a small mop. Keep the fingers clear of this mixture, as it is poisonous.

OIL-POLISHING AND WAX-POLISHING

OIL-POLISHING FURNITURE—FLOORS—WAX-POLISHING FURNITURE AND FLOORS

FOR the method of oil-polishing little instruction is necessary. It is simplicity itself, and yet it is a form of polishing which must not be overlooked, as it has its advantages over French polishing, wax-polishing, or varnishing. There is no fear of an oil-polished surface cracking or blistering, like either French polish or varnish; nor will it show marks, especially marks made with water, as does wax-polish. To do the work requires a great deal of time, and a considerable amount of friction in its application. It is most used on plain surfaces, owing to the amount of rubbing which is needed to do the work in a proper manner.

The Treatment is similar to wax-polishing, and consists of rubbing oil into the wood with a soft rag. But it must not be confounded with mere oiling, which is chiefly employed to bring out the figure of the wood prior to French polishing, and which consists of nothing more than a mere wipe over the work with raw oil. In the case of oil-polishing, the oil is vigorously rubbed into the work, and the application must be continued at intervals, preferably daily, for some five or six weeks if a good job is required. Either boiled or raw linseed oil may be used, and the rubbing at each application must continue until the surface is dry. When this has taken place daily for a few weeks the result will be a most durable surface, and comparatively dull as regards gloss. This gives a fine effect, especially on oak.

Oil-polishing is most useful for table tops, bar tables, counters and spirit cabinets. A dining-room table with an oil-polished top, and the sides and legs French polished,

Staining and Polishing

will make a most satisfactory job. Of course the legs and framework could be oil-polished if desired, but it is unnecessary. If the top is French polished it is liable to become marked and seriously damaged if hot dishes are placed upon it, whilst the same hot dishes may be placed upon the table with impunity if it has been oil-polished.

To prepare the Oil, put the required quantity into a vessel over a fire or stove, and gently simmer (not boil) for a quarter of an hour. Then take it off and add one-eighth of turpentine. For a table-top or other surface which is large and level, rub some of the oil well into it, and then polish with a rubber made by rubbing a quantity of felt or flannel round a brick or other suitable block, the purpose of which is, by its weight, to relieve to some extent the polisher from using his muscles in applying pressure. In applying the oil to the wood do not saturate or flood it, but scrub it in, and afterwards rub long and hard. Of course the wood will absorb the oil, even after several applications. It will need much patience to bring it up to a good glow; in fact, it might be said that the work is never finished. An oiled surface will always bear more rubbing than it has had, and will not deteriorate by friction. It can always be rubbed over again at any time with the oil, and will be improved by so doing.

In pure Oil-polishing linseed oil is the only medium used, but other ingredients have been employed till it is difficult sometimes to recognise the distinction between oil-polishing and French polishing. The two processes may overlap to an almost indefinite extent, but we do not intend to go into that matter, as it will only have a tendency to confuse the novice. The reason that turpentine is usually added to the oil is because it helps it to dry quicker than it would otherwise do. Some polishers recommend boiled linseed oil, others raw, while yet others will advise various proportions of the two. The reader can rest assured that whichever he adopts he will be perfectly safe in his choice,

Oil-Polishing and Wax-Polishing

as there is really not much difference between the two oils as regards this kind of work. If, after a good polish has been obtained, the work begins to sweat, rub some methylated spirits in. This will dry the surface without spoiling the polish.

In polishing Open-grained Woods, they can be filled up in the ordinary way with a grain-filler, and afterwards polished as directed. The oil should be applied with either soft rag or a piece of flannel. Each time the oil is applied the surface should be previously washed with cold water to remove any dirt or dust. Care should be taken to see that a good brand of turpentine is used to mix with the oil, as if a cheap brand or a turpentine substitute is used trouble is likely to ensue. Turpentine substitutes are now exceedingly common on the market (owing to the cost of pure turpentine being so high), and some of them contain a fair percentage of oils of the petroleum class, which is apt to dry up the linseed oil and act on the surface of the wood as a bleaching agent. The work may also turn very dull as a consequence. Several applications of hot oil should do much to restore the work to its former state. If the wood is mahogany, red oil should be used, as this will readily bring back the brightness of the colour of the wood. Of course it cannot be used on any wood except red woods, so that other woods should have the oil slightly tinted to suit the local colour.

In polishing Spirit Cabinets—bar tables and counters must be included in this category—oil-polish is far superior to ordinary French polish. The latter being simply shellac, or other gums dissolved in methylated spirits or wood naphtha, it gives a surface that is readily softened by alcohol. An oil-varnish finish would be better than a French-polish finish, but a high grade, tough, yet hard-drying oil-varnish must be used; and even then this will eventually yield to the action of spirits or hot glasses. The best possible finish for this class of goods is undoubtedly

Staining and Polishing

oil-polishing. Spirits cannot soften up the surface, nor will hot glasses mark it. Only such portions of the work as are subject to the action of spirits or hot glasses or dishes will need to be oil-polished; the rest may be finished in any desired manner—French polish, wax-polish, varnish, or any other known method of finishing woodwork.

A quicker method than full oil-polishing may be resorted to, especially when time must be taken into consideration, and this would be to use a grain-filler, body up with ordinary French polish, and then grind down with felt and pumice powder, using either oil or water for the purpose. Afterwards the work may be oil-polished in the usual way, but it will not require very many applications of the oil to effect the desired finish. It should, however, be freshened up occasionally with the oil-polish so as to maintain a surface that will withstand the action of the spirits. Another method is to body up with French polish, and finish off with a waterproof polish. But neither of these methods, it may be mentioned, is equal in durability to complete oil-polishing.

Floors.—Another use to which oil-polishing may be put is as a finish for floors or floor margins. It is not, however, commonly resorted to for this kind of work, but still it is a very valuable treatment where a dull finish is required. It will not tread off as varnish and French polish are apt to do, nor will it be affected by washing, as wax-polishing is. The only objection is in regard to the amount of labour required to bring it up to a respectable polish, and the need for freshening up occasionally. Otherwise it is to be recommended as a polish that will wear well and not mark readily. The floors are stained in the usual manner, generally oak or walnut being the woods imitated for this purpose. The staining is done in the ordinary manner, and preferably sized to ensure equal absorption for the after-coats.

Ballroom Floors are polished with beeswax and tur-

Oil-Polishing and Wax-Polishing

pentine in the ordinary manner, and, to keep them in good order, powdered wax and a little French chalk are sprinkled upon them from time to time. For the temporary polishing of a floor to be used for dancing, use powdered wax and French chalk. The French chalk must be used sparingly so as to avoid excessive dust.

WAX-POLISHING.

The process of wax-polishing, a very simple and easy one, is capable of yielding excellent results. It is quite as simple as oil-polishing, but requires more energy in its application. In appearance it is somewhat similar to a good oil-polished surface, but it is done more quickly. Any wood may be wax-polished, though it is not often that other than oak or mahogany is so finished. The effect obtained by this kind of polishing is exceedingly rich, owing to its fine eggshell gloss. It is perhaps most appropriate—and certainly most used—for polishing fumed oak, when it possesses an attractiveness not even shared by French polish. For antique furniture—whether genuine or not—it is the best finish, giving the work a more ancient appearance than varnish will do. Mahogany also is often so treated, and for many purposes the process may be considered superior to French polish which has been dulled. Wax-polishing is also particularly suitable for wood stained black to imitate ebony, as it is a closer approximation to real ebony than when French polished.

The Ingredients for wax-polish vary slightly, but the general and also the simplest mixture is composed of beeswax and turpentine. Resin is sometimes added to harden the polish, but it is better without. Venice turpentine is also sometimes used in the mixture, in conjunction with a certain proportion of resin. The simple mixture of beeswax and turpentine is, however, sufficient for ordinary purposes, and is therefore recommended for general work. There is both yellow and white wax, and the reader must

Staining and Polishing

decide for himself which to use ; some prefer the white, whilst others always use the yellow variety. It may be said that there is no special reason why white wax should be used in preference to yellow, unless it be where white woods are desired to be waxed. In such circumstances the white variety would unquestionably be the better one to use, but as white woods are very seldom waxed this point need not be laboured. In cases where a cheaper and quicker method than the usual one outlined below is desired, another kind of wax should be employed. This is called paraffin wax, and although not a true wax it is now largely used in place of the more expensive beeswax. It is the wax that is employed in the manufacture of the common wax candle, so that the economical reader may take advantage of this note.

To make the Preparation, the wax—which is obtained in cakes—should be shredded as fine as possible. It may be made with the help of heat to accelerate the process, or may be done by what might be termed the cold process. In the latter case the wax is simply shredded into the cold turpentine and left to dissolve without any interference, except perhaps an occasional stir with a stick. This takes some time for the wax to dissolve thoroughly, but nevertheless it will dissolve all right in this way and there is not the same attendant risk that is experienced in the other method. If the worker places the wax in the turpentine in the evening it will be ready for use next day.

In the other method—namely the application of heat to assist the wax to dissolve—there is some danger. There are, however, two or three ways of doing it, the most common, and no doubt the best, being to heat the dry wax first until thoroughly dissolved, and then to add the turpentine gradually and before the wax has stiffened. The vessel containing the wax should be much deeper than the bulk of wax, or it may catch fire. Another point to note is to take the vessel off the fire or stove when pouring in the turpentine, as turpentine is very inflammable, and a few drops

Oil-Polishing and Wax-Polishing

accidentally poured over the side of the vessel would cause a big and dangerous blaze.

A less dangerous method is to stand the wax and turpentine in hot water, and obtain the necessary heat in that way. Instead of melting the wax only, both the wax and turpentine may be put in and heated up together, but this will necessitate careful watching, and the safest way is to adopt the method outlined above.

Resin and Wax.—If a mixture is required with resin as one of the ingredients, the resin should be melted first and the wax then added, a little at a time, the mixture being stirred during the process. The mixture should not be applied hot, but must be allowed to cool before use. Of course it will stiffen in the cooling, and if it is found to be too stiff for the purpose required, it may be warmed up again and more turpentine added. If on the other hand it is found to be too thin, melt some more wax—stiffer this time—and add to the first mixture; the latter should, however, be warmed slightly for the purpose of intermixture, as the two will then amalgamate better.

Consistency.—If a very stiff paste is used the wax will very probably be deposited in excessive quantity, which will necessitate a great amount of rubbing to remove it. There is the risk of the work being left ridgy, through an uneven distribution of the wax. A polish that is fluid will be spread much more evenly, but no gloss will be obtained until the turpentine has evaporated somewhat. This evaporation will not take very long, so that a number of coats could be given, and as the polish would be spread more evenly it is a better plan than having the mixture too stiff. Everything depends upon the nature of the surface to be polished; an open-grained wood will need a rather stiff paste, while for a close-grained wood a polish of the consistency of thick cream would be the best. A paste of the consistency of butter in hot weather might be safely regarded as a medium.

Applying the Wax.—The wax is applied with a piece

Staining and Polishing

of rag or a brush. Some polishers prefer one and some the other. The main factor is to have the polish evenly distributed, the manipulation of the rubbers being of secondary importance. As with all polishing, the required finish is obtained by friction, and with wax-polishing plenty of hard rubbing is required; but the stiffer the paste the harder will the rubbing be. The surface to be polished is better if new, or if it is old work it should be free from furniture paste or dirt of any description.

On new work particular note must be taken to see that the wood is thoroughly dry, as if it is damp an effective polish will not be obtained. The same thing applies to the rag or brush employed in the polishing, which must be perfectly free from damp or moisture. Three rubbers should be used for this process, one for applying the paste, another for scrubbing it up fairly bright, and the third for finishing off with. The first is usually a piece of coarse rag; the second rubber, by which the real polishing is done, should preferably be a brush, as more friction can be applied to the work than would be the case were a rag used. Some polishers use a piece of flannel or baize, or similar material. Each polisher has his own idea as to which is the better and the reader must decide the question for himself.

Finishing-off is done with a clean dry cloth, the rubbing being continued till the surface is as bright as it can be got. If, after having done some polishing, there is a quantity of the paste left, it should be kept for future use in a tightly-corked bottle or airtight canister, as otherwise the turpentine will evaporate and the mass get hard.

New Woods, particularly the open-grained ones (like oak, for instance), need many applications to get a really satisfactory result. It is not usual to use a grain-filler on wax-polished furniture. The charm of wax-polishing lies in the old-fashioned appearance that it gives to the article, and this is destroyed to a great extent if the grain is filled up as in French polishing. But if there is a special reason

Oil-Polishing and Wax-Polishing

why the grain should appear full, cornflour may be added to the wax mixture, more turpentine being added to bring it to a working consistency. This may, however, cause the

CARVED PICTURE FRAME—GOTHIC STYLE.

surface to appear rather dull at first, but brightness may be imparted by using more wax, free from flour, after the filling-in mixture has had time to harden. Some polishers

Staining and Polishing

will French polish the wood to fill the grain before applying the wax. The polish is applied until the grain is nicely filled, then allowed to harden, and the surface afterwards dulled down by means of pumice powder. The work is then waxed, the process giving to the wood a fine antique or eggshell finish.

CARVED PIPE RACK.

Renovating.—Wax-polished surfaces may be renovated at any time by simply giving them another rub over with the same kind of mixture. The state of the weather will guide the operator as to whether the polish should be applied warm or not; in cold weather warming will be found to facilitate matters very much.

Floors.—In wax-polishing a floor a weighted brush with a long swivel handle is used, and this is manipulated by the operator standing in the middle of the floor, taking long sweeps on either side. Ronuk is a special preparation most suitable for floors. Wax-polished floors cannot be washed, but must be wiped over or rubbed with a dry cloth. The paste may be stained to any colour, provided oil stainers are used for the purpose. By this means surfaces may be both stained and waxed at one process. Any cracks or nail holes may be filled up with pure wax, or with ordinary putty.

STENCILLING ON WOOD AND ORNAMENTAL WOOD STAINING

STENCILLING is the application of a pattern by means of brushing paint over a perforated plate. The design is cut out of some thin material, such as paper or zinc; a pigment is brushed over the plate with short stiff brushes, made expressly for this purpose, called stencil brushes (Fig. 31), and the colour passing through the stencil plate leaves an impression on the surface of the work. The perforated plate or paper is called

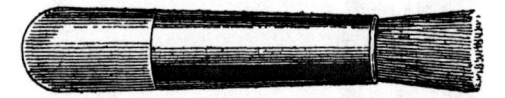

FIG. 31.—STENCIL BRUSH.

a stencil. A simple stencil and the impression made with it are shown in Figs. 32 and 33. In the stencil shown the parts cut away are indicated in white; in the impression the stencilled parts are indicated in black. In the design it will be noticed that the leaves and petals of the flower do not run into each other, but that a narrow portion is left between, just where they would in ordinary course meet. These narrow pieces are called "ties," and they must not be forgotten when cutting out the design. These ties have a two-fold object, to strengthen the stencil plate and to enable a true representation of the desired ornament to be given.

As an example, take the letter A. Cut the two side lines out first, and then the horizontal line half-way down the letter, and the result when stencilled would appear as shown in Fig. 34. The centre of the letter would drop away, and though you would have the correct outside shape of the

Staining and Polishing

letter, the impression you wished to convey would be entirely lost. Instead of cutting the horizontal line right across from one upright to the other, a narrow piece should be cut at either end, and also one at the top of the letter. This will serve the purpose of holding the top space of the letter in position, and will not interfere with the production of a correct representation of the letter (see Fig. 34). In the

FIG. 32.—STENCIL PLATE.

FIG. 33.—IMPRESSION FROM PLATE.

same way there must be ties in all stencils, but they must not be placed *anywhere*. The correct place is just where the lines join or meet. Figs. 35, 36, and 37 show the best places for ties.

CUTTING A STENCIL.—Let us now take a design and prepare to cut it out. First of all, draw the desired design on a sheet of good strong paper, preferably cartridge paper. Zinc is sometimes used, but it is not to be recommended, for if it gets bent in any way it can never be restored to its original position. Moreover, cartridge paper is cheaper, is easier to cut and manipulate, and will give better results.

Stencilling on Wood and Wood Staining

Place the paper on a sheet of glass—or, if glass is not available, on a sheet of block tin or some other hard and perfectly

FIG. 34.—CUTTING A STENCIL LETTER A.

FIG. 35.—TIES ON A STENCIL.

FIG. 36.    FIG. 37.    FIG. 38.

smooth surface—and cut the design out with a stencil knife, as shown in Fig. 38. A small pocket-knife shaped at the end like those in Fig. 39, and perfectly sharp and clean, will answer the purpose very well. In cutting out always

Staining and Polishing

cut away from the corners (Fig. 38), and so avoid the risk of slipping across the ties.

After finishing the cutting out, give the stencil plate on both sides a coat of shellac varnish, called by painters "knotting." This will prevent the stains from softening the paper, and will keep it firm.

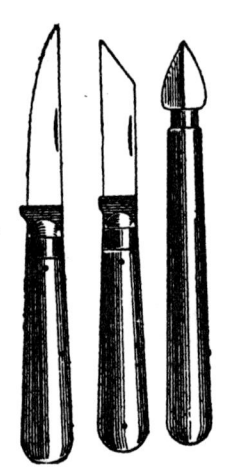

FIG. 39.—STENCIL KNIVES.

FIG. 40.—STENCILLED PATTERN WITH LONG STALK.

Pour a little of the stain in a saucer or other shallow vessel, and have a piece of brown paper close by in which to lightly dab the brush when taking up more colour from the saucer. This is to distribute the colour evenly over the bristles, and prevent the stain from running when applied to the stencil, as might happen if there were too much colour in the brush.

With drawing-pins fasten the stencil plate on to the wood it is wished to decorate, and, with the brush in the right hand, hold the stencil firmly to the wood with the left hand, keeping down with the fingers any parts that may happen to stick up through not having sufficient ties to keep them

Stencilling on Wood and Wood Staining

flat. In this manner and with a little practice it should be easy to make a nice, clean-edged design.

When artistic stencils are employed, it is sometimes desirable to obliterate the breaks, or ties, from the patterns, as, for instance, when they occur in a long stalk (Fig. 40). To accomplish this, another stencil which contains only the ties is cut, and this is passed over the pattern, from which the breaks are obliterated with the brush. It is necessary that the tie-stencil should fit accurately over the design which has already been coloured, for if the ties are irregularly blotted out the symmetry of the design will of course be destroyed. The ties could of course be filled up by hand, but the work must be very carefully done, and the result is not nearly so good.

ORNAMENTAL WOOD STAINING.

The Art of ornamental staining, with simple instructions for the carrying out of the various processes may now be considered.

TO LEAVE A PLAIN WOOD PATTERN ON A STAINED GROUND.

First Method.—A pattern may be entirely cut out of lining paper and gummed or pasted to the panel. This is not a question of stencilling, as the design is cut clean out of the paper, and only the design is pasted to the panel. Every precaution should be taken to prevent the gum or paste from soiling any portion of the panel other than that covered by the paper. The paper itself must be well sized before the pattern is cut out of it. When the paper has dried, the panel may be oil stained, the paper protecting those portions of the wood that it covers. When the oil stain is dry a little soaking with water will remove the paper, leaving a clean wood pattern upon a stained ground.

Staining and Polishing

The paste or gum prevents the oil stain from running underneath the paper.

A similar method is used when fumigating oak; the covered portions of the work do not take the fume, and various patterns can be produced on the work. The paper pattern or stencil may be fixed on the oak work by coating the paper with thick heavy white polish. Some workers pick out the work by applying liquid paraffin wax with a pencil brush. The portions coated with the wax solution will not be penetrated by the ammonia fumes.

Second Method.—This method requires the use of the stencil. Draw and cut a design according to the instructions already given on stencilling. Place the plate on the panel, and stencil the design in spirit varnish or knotting. Take the plate off immediately after execution, and allow the spirit varnish to dry, which will not take more than a few minutes. When quite dry stain the whole of the panel over with a water-stain. The varnish design will resist the water, the remainder of the panel only taking the stain. When the latter is dry, wipe off the stain from the design with a piece of wash-leather, and there is left a clear wood pattern upon a stained ground.

TO PUT SOLID COLOUR ON A WATER-STAINED GROUND, OR ON PLAIN WOOD.

Coat the Panel with glue-size—a material which can be bought prepared from any druggist, colourman, or painter—and when dry decorate in any desired manner, either by stencil or by hand, with opaque oil colours. When this is dry the size must be washed off with warm water, after which the panel can be stained with various stains in water, the stain over the oil painting being wiped off when dry with a wash-leather. If desired the panel may be left unstained, in which case the size would not be washed off, and the varnishing or polishing could be proceeded with directly the design was dry.

Stencilling on Wood and Wood Staining

TO EXECUTE A PATTERN WITH DARK OUTLINE.

Draw the Design upon ordinary drawing-paper, and proceed to prick in the design with a hatpin; that is, place the paper upon a shawl or similar article, and push the pin through the paper on to the lines of the pattern, allowing the holes to be about $\frac{1}{8}$ in. apart. Next obtain some powdered whiting, and put about an egg-cupful in a piece of fine muslin, tying it up in the shape of a ball. Now fasten the drawing to the panel or other object to be decorated, and dab over all the pinholes with the bag of powdered whiting. Take the paper off the wood, and the pattern will be outlined on the panel in small specks of whiting. With a fine pencil (a small brush) outline the design in oil colour of a dark shade, and when dry stain in between the lines with either oil, spirit, or water-stains. The dark lines in oil will prevent the various stains from striking against each other.

A PATTERN WITH LIGHT OUTLINE ON WATER-STAIN.

First size the panel twice. Then go through the same process of pouncing the design on the panel, as instructed in the previous paragraph. This time, however, outline in Brunswick black. This will quickly dry; then wash off the size and stain with water-stains, both inside and outside of design. When quite dry, remove the Brunswick black with a free use of turpentine and clean rag. The result will be a clear wood outline on a stained pattern and ground.

TO OBTAIN A POLYCHROMATIC EFFECT.

A pattern may be stencilled in knotting or spirit varnish, and a little colour of a lighter shade of the intended ground colour added to the knotting or varnish will produce a polychromatic effect.

Staining and Polishing

A STENCIL OF BLENDED STAINS.

A Stencil may be put upon the bare wood in deep rich varnish stains, blended by stencilling. This means that portions of the design are stencilled in with one colour, and while wet the design is completed with another colour, dabbing the latter colour a little way into the first one. This, if done smartly, produces a beautiful effect, showing all the gradations of tone from the one colour into the other. When the varnish is dry stain with a water-stain.

OBTAINING DIFFERENT DEPTHS OF STAIN IN WATER ON ONE PANEL.

Stain all the panel in first with the lightest stain it is intended to use, and when dry give the portions you wish to remain in this colour a coat of white hard varnish. Again stain all the panel, this time with the next deeper stain, and coat the portions required to stay in this colour with a coat of the same varnish. Then stain all over with the next deeper stain, and varnish the desired portions of this stain; and so on until the whole of the stains are in. Finally, remove the varnish with methylated spirits and a sponge, which will leave the stain unaffected. Then varnish or polish.

These ideas can be extended and elaborated, and can be used in conjunction with each other to advantage. Their scope is limited only by the invention and resource of the student. The choice of colours is important, but no attempt is made here to give any colour scheme, for to ensure satisfaction one must be in a position to know the colour and nature of objects immediately surrounding the work in hand.

VARNISH

The Uses of Varnish—Making Varnish—Classes of Varnish

THERE are many occasions when the use of polish—French, wax, or otherwise—will not produce a coating with sufficient protective power and brilliancy, or when it is desired to coat some surface at less expense than is entailed by polishing. On occasions such as these varnishing is resorted to, and this process may be either a cheap one utilising a single coat of common varnish, or it may take the form of the high glaze on carriage work which is the result of many very carefully applied coats of the very best material.

WHAT VARNISH IS.

Varnish is a material of transparent appearance, and is used either as a preservative agent or as a means of obtaining a high finish. Varnishes are sometimes coloured by reason of their composition, as in black japan; or by the addition of dye-stuffs, as in lacquers. Japans and enamels are admixtures of varnish and colouring matter, sometimes in a transparent and sometimes in a more or less opaque form. As these latter-mentioned materials will be dealt with later on, we do not intend to dwell upon them at this stage. The value of varnish as a protective or a preservative agent is sufficiently well known to need no emphasis here. Perhaps no other material of a similar character can surpass it in value for this kind of work.

Modern Varnish is manufactured on a large scale, and unfortunately a good deal is not of a quality that carries recommendation with it. On the contrary, it is mainly made to be used and to be renewed, and much work to which it is applied is neither decorated nor preserved as it

Staining and Polishing

should be. Thoroughly good varnish properly applied (and there is much art in this) becomes indeed a lasting preservative, besides adding enormously to the beauty of the article thus treated, especially in the case of finely-wrought woods.

Properly speaking, varnish may technically be described as a solution of any resinous material in a solvent, alcohol and oils being the usual ones employed. It is important that the solution should be thin and fluid, and it ought to be easily capable of being spread evenly over any surface; while, by the use of colouring substances such as, say, gamboge, turmeric, saffron, dragon's blood, etc., beautiful tints of yellow, brown and red, etc., can be given, so as to render the varnish highly decorative.

But when we consider that the staple materials used, such as gum copal and other well-known varnish gums, vary in price by pounds sterling per cwt., that the quality of the linseed oils used is of very special importance—for on that depends much of the beauty of the resultant varnish—and that the methods of making differ greatly, it is clear enough that the choice of a good varnish is not the easy thing that some think it is. Varnishes for paintings, high-class cabinet work, and for fittings generally, all differ greatly, and many valuable productions that have cost invention, skill and labour are ruined because of inattention to the finishing off with a varnish that shall lie on the surface thin, perfectly transparent, and of a diamond hardness, capable of being readily cleaned and of resisting the effects of time indefinitely, as an ideal varnish does.

The Use of Varnish is of a two-fold nature—first, the preservation of, and second, giving additional beauty to, the object it is used upon. In order to obtain the best results it is necessary to use the best materials, and also to know the suitability of the varnish to the article or articles to be varnished, as well as the various influences affecting these.

Varnish

The Materials Used in the making of varnishes are various gums, resins, etc., dissolved in linseed, cotton-seed, or nut oils, spirits of turpentine, methylated spirit, or wood naphtha, either by a cold process or the application of heat. The quality, durability and beauty of the higher-class varnishes is dependent upon the greatest care, both in the selection of materials and their skilful manipulation in the process of manufacture. Many of the most popular varnishes also are kept for longer or shorter periods to "mature" before being sent out to customers, and all varnish manufacturers of note keep a careful register of the date when boiled, bulked and bottled—the date always appearing on the label, the age adding to its value.

The Best Quality of varnish is made from the finest selected fossil resin and the purest refined Baltic linseed oil, at a carefully regulated and steady heat over sand-bath protected furnaces to prevent its firing, and is used for high-class decorations, carriage, and other work, when cost is not the first consideration. It is a slow dryer, but is of great lustre and durability. It should be applied in a room of uniform temperature of from 70° to 75°, from which all draughts must be rigidly excluded.

A very high-class varnish is made from selected gum copal, with a small addition of gum damar (to give elasticity), oil and turpentine. It is used on good-class work, is suitable for decorators, etc., and is equally applicable for inside or outside work.

The various Lower-class Varnishes are made from the same kinds of gums, oils, etc., of lower grades and darker shades, with the addition of common resin, cotton, rape, fish, and other oils, and the cheaper spirits, such as coal-tar spirit, mineral naphtha (rectified petroleum) and benzolene as adulterants. These find purchasers mainly amongst tradespeople and others whose chief object is to get the maximum quantity at a minimum cost. Their

Staining and Polishing

qualities, like everything else of the "cheap" kind, are poor, and the varnishes dear at any price.

MAKING VARNISH.

It is rarely worth while for the home worker to make his own varnish, but (if care is exercised to prevent accident from fire) it can be made on a small scale.

Gum Copal.—For the base of a fine varnish African gum copal can be recommended. It should be bought well scraped; and for really choice work pick out the most transparent pieces, which ought to be like drops of crystal. These should be reduced into very small parts, and it is best to dry them in the sun, this being preferable to fire heat. Then, when dry, pound some into powder and boil in soft water (rainwater is the best). Now take clean broken glass and soda. After bruising the lot into very small particles, boil and strain away the moisture. Repeat this until there is no impurity left. When the broken glass is quite dry—in fact a powder—mix it with the powdered copal, previously dried, in the proportion of 2 to 3, blend the whole, put them into a vessel and fuse the gum, stirring well. The reduced glass prevents the gum from massing. When the gum is reduced to a fluid state, add clarified oil, say 3 quarts to 5 lbs. of gum and glass, and boil till it strings quite freely on taking a little up on the finger. Next add 5 quarts of turpentine, strain and pour it into (preferably) a big glass bottle. Leave the top open and exposed to air, but not to sunshine, and be sure to keep it perfectly dry. Let it age and it will be found splendid varnish for the finest artistic work.

Linseed Oil.—The choice of linseed oil is of great importance in the case of the resultant varnish, whether for fine or ordinary uses. If the oil be made, as not a little is, from *unripe* seeds, it will necessarily abound with particles of a more or less acidulous character, and will

Varnish

not yield good results. The quality of linseed oil can generally be determined by the following means: Fill a small bottle with the oil to be tested and hold it up to a strong light. Now, if that oil is not good, it is more or less opaque and thick; moreover, if it has an acid flavour to the taste, and if it smells at all strong, reject it at once. Fine-grade oil, made from properly ripened seed, when looked at through glass against the light, is pale, limpid and brilliant. Moreover, it has very little smell at all, and it will be rather sweet to the taste. Another thing to note particularly is that pure oil is always much lighter than the impure article. It does not add perceptibly to the colour of the varnish and it always dries quickly.

Turpentine.—It is equally important to have really good turpentine. Unfortunately, turpentine and turpentine substitutes vary greatly in quality, and that of a low grade will inevitably spoil fine varnishes. Turpentine should be entirely free from acids. That coming from the resin of green trees has a quantity of pernicious pyroligneous acid. It is easily detected, as it is bitter to the taste and precipitates into a milky substance. The longer that turpentine is kept before making into varnish the better, if the bottom portion is not used.

To resist Boiling Water.—A good varnish for woodwork to resist boiling water is made of linseed oil, pulverised litharge and pulverised white lead, boiled together with some minium (red lead) and a little amber. There are, however, a great variety of varnishes for special purposes. Thus for violins a really beautiful varnish can be made from equal parts of coarsely-powdered gum copal and glass, alcohol, and a little camphor. Then a golden varnish is made by the addition of saffron and dragon's blood, which, properly made and skilfully applied, will seem almost as beautiful as though the surface thus treated were actually gilded.

It might here be pointed out that the more delicate the

Staining and Polishing

tint, shade, or colour of the object to be varnished, the paler must be the varnish, or otherwise much well-finished work will be spoiled. It is also a mistake to use a dark, opaque varnish upon such self-colours as blue, green, red or black, as it nearly always produces a muddy or blurred finish. Mixed, medium, or "broken" colours are almost the only permissible cases in which these varnishes should be used. Should a varnish prove brittle or too quick in use, the addition of a very small quantity of linseed oil may be allowed; if fatty or too thick with age or exposure to air, use a little turpentine, but in all cases where practicable use it intact.

CLASSES OF VARNISH—WATER, SPIRIT AND OIL.

Varnishes may be divided into three classes—water, spirit, and oil, according to the vehicle employed in the process of making. Water varnishes are gums, etc., dissolved in water. Spirit varnishes are gums or resins dissolved in spirits. Oil varnishes are gums or resins dissolved in oils.

Water Varnishes are composed of gum-arabic or isinglass dissolved in water, and are mostly used for the protection of paper. There are also shellac water varnishes. Shellac is not soluble in water, therefore borax or other ingredients are added to make these varnishes.

Spirit Varnishes include the French polishes, white and brown hard spirit varnish, japanners' varnish, paper varnish (for use on wall papers), patent knotting, and flatting varnish—a varnish that dries without gloss. All quick-drying varnishes—from French polish to floor stains—are, more or less, spirit, and are made (or should be) by dissolving shellac, sandarac, or other brittle gum, in turpentine or methylated spirit. Spirit varnish is used principally upon furniture, floors, and for other domestic purposes. A finer

Varnish

class is also used (on account of the hardness of its surface) for pianos and office and other heavy furniture requiring much handling. There is also a spirit varnish used for wallpapers, prints, maps, etc.—all of which require to be sized before applying the varnish, which should be made with the softer gums and turpentines by the application of heat.

Spirit varnishes are of three kinds, viz.: bleached hard, a colourless varnish; white hard, white in colour and not so transparent as the bleached variety; and brown hard, a dark brown varnish for use on dark-coloured woods. All these contain methylated spirit as a solvent, and are of a quick-drying, lustrous nature. Ether varnish, as its name implies, contains ether instead of spirit, and, consequently dries quicker than methylated varnish. Naphtha varnish is another very quick-drying varnish, wood naphtha being used as the vehicle for dissolving the gums. It is more commonly used on builders' work, such as fronts of shops, hand-rails, etc. Varnishes can also be obtained coloured, or can be coloured by the addition of liquid spirit stains.

Oil Varnishes may be divided into white oil varnishes, pale oil varnishes, medium oil varnishes, dark oil varnishes, and mastic varnish. This last is mostly used for paintings and pictures of value. Amongst the white oil varnishes may be mentioned white marble varnish, Coburg, French oil, etc., these being used for the best kind of internal work. The pale oil varnishes include maple varnish, pale copal, and pale carriage varnish. The medium oil varnishes may be known by the names of carriage, pale oak, etc., and are made suitable for either indoor or external work. The dark oil varnishes are generally known by the names of church oak, hard oak, etc., and these also are manufactured for both inside and outside work.

Oil varnishes dry, not by evaporation like spirit varnishes, but by oxidisation; that is, the oil in the varnish absorbs oxygen from the air, and solidifies the oil with the gum, thereby forming a skin of a preservative character.

Staining and Polishing

A certain amount of evaporation does take place, however, as some proportion of spirit (generally turpentine) is usually added to the oil varnishes to make them more easily workable. But the best class of varnishes contain very little of this spirit element, and are consequently slow-drying varnishes.

Natural Varnishes.—In addition to the above there are also what might be termed natural varnishes, as india-rubber solution, lacquers, etc. Lacquers and spirit varnishes dry and harden by the evaporation of the volatile spirit, thus leaving the gum or resin as a thin shell over the surface of the work.

HARD AND ELASTIC VARNISHES.

Varnishes may be subdivided into hard and elastic varnishes. Of course there is no strict line between the two qualities, for there is hardly a varnish of the hard type which does not possess a certain amount of elasticity; and there is not an elastic varnish which does not possess the quality of hardness, even though it may be comparatively infinitesimal. Then between the two extremes we get varnishes possessing varying degrees of hardness and elasticity, until we arrive at some which it would be a difficult matter to determine to which class they really belong.

Generally speaking, the spirit varnishes belong to the hard class, as do also the majority of the dark oil varnishes such as church oak, dark oak, hard oak, etc. The paler the oil varnishes the more elastic they are as a rule. These latter are usually made from gum copal, which is a clear and very elastic gum.

The Hard Varnishes are made either from resins or from gums which are more resinous in their nature. These will not stand hard wear, and should not be used where subject to sunlight or the outside air.

Varnish

It is not safe to use a hard varnish either under or over an elastic one. Hard varnishes do not give much "key" for the subsequent coats, and therefore the latter will not have the hold upon the ground that they really should have. If, on the other hand, a hard varnish is placed directly upon an elastic one, it will inevitably crack and crawl, owing to the elastic varnish underneath "pulling" in various directions.

The Elastic Varnishes are particularly suitable for outside wear, being yielding enough to contract and expand with the changes of the temperature to which they are subjected. They should therefore be used on all articles or interior surfaces which are near the window or the door. Readers may have noticed varnish round the inside of windows very badly cracked, while the rest of the varnish in the room is in good condition. This is because a hard varnish has been used, and has suffered where it is in contact with the sunlight.

When there is any doubt as to the comparative hardness of two varnishes which have to be used one under the other, it is a fairly safe plan to add a small percentage of turpentine to the under one, or as an alternative to rub it out very sparingly and allow it to harden thoroughly for at least a week before finishing. When uncertain as to the nature of the varnishes about to be used, apply the following test: Procure two pieces of tin, and give a coat of each varnish to the different pieces of tin, allow them to harden for a day or two, and then scratch with the thumb-nail to see which is harder, or bend the tin to see which is more elastic.

Varnish for Church Seats.—When choosing a varnish for church seats, it should be remembered that it not only has to be handled very much, but that it also has to undergo the stewing of the heated and moist atmosphere charged with the breath of overcrowded congregations. For an oil varnish to stand this, it should be of a very hard drying

Staining and Polishing

quality. Most of the varnishes provided for church seats have been manufactured to suit the damp and cold climate of a country where the clamminess of a hot summer's night is comparatively unknown. These varnishes do not always dry hard enough for church seats elsewhere. If the seats are new, it is well to keep all oil varnish off them, or to use only the best hard drying carriage varnish. A better plan is to polish them or use spirit varnish. The heat of the hands or the heat of a crowded room will tend to make even the hardest oil varnish sticky.

To properly prepare seats for revarnishing, where the old varnish has become black with handling and fluffy from stickiness, the old stuff should be removed with a paint remover, or with a solution of caustic soda, and the whole begun afresh. It is little use putting on a good hard drying varnish on the top of one that remains sticky. The old must be removed or made to dry. Sometimes the varnish underneath may be made to dry by rubbing it down with turpentine. A coat of hard drying carriage varnish may then be applied.

If spirit varnish is put on the top of a soft oil varnish it is sure to crack, and the same effect is likely to take place if a hard drying varnish is put over a sticky surface. The best way is to clean the whole of the old stuff off and begin afresh, taking care that the seats are dry and clean before applying the first coat.

VARNISHING

SURFACES FOR VARNISHING—BRUSHES—APPLYING VARNISH—FELTING DOWN—SPIRIT VARNISHING, ETC.

APART from the selection of the right kind of varnish, there are other factors to be considered if success in varnishing is to be attained. The conditions necessary to ensure satisfactory work are numerous, and one of the most important conditions is cleanliness. It matters not how particular you may have been in choosing the right varnish for the job, or what care you may have exercised in bringing the work up thus far; unless the rule with regard to cleanliness has been scrupulously observed the result is certain to be disappointing.

New Wood.—Varnishing cannot take place upon *any* kind of ground. We will take, for instance, new wood. Here the main consideration is the number of coats of varnish that the work is to receive. If the job will allow of any number of coats being applied, provided that the result is good, then we might with advantage dispense with any kind of preparation. But if the work is to receive only a limited number of coats—say two, or perhaps three—then we must apply some method of stopping undue suction of the wood in places and make it more even, otherwise the work will appear when finished very bright in some places while dull in others. This unevenness of gloss is caused through the unequal absorption of the varnish by the new wood. It therefore follows that if this is to be guarded against the wood must receive a coat of some preparation to effect this object.

For this purpose glue-size may be used, made up as explained on page 12. This should be applied prior to any varnishing, and care exercised to see that no superfluous size is left on the edges or in quirks or mouldings. Too much size will damage the varnish and affect the gloss. The preser-

Staining and Polishing

vation of the wood is best ensured by giving it a coat of varnish on the unprepared surface ; then a coat of isinglass size is applied and the varnishing is again proceeded with.

Painted Work.—In varnishing on painted work some little knowledge of painting is essential. To produce the best results the last coat of paint should be what is termed in the trade " flat " ; that is, it should be dead, or without gloss. Paint is mixed with linseed oil and with turpentine to make it workable. The more oil there is put into the paint the greater will be the gloss when dry. The more turpentine is added the flatter the paint becomes. Therefore to get the last coat of paint dead, it should be mixed almost entirely with turpentine.

If a greater proportion of oil has been mixed with the paint than should have been the case, then the oiliness may be removed by washing the work down with fuller's earth and water. Dissolve about 1 oz. of fuller's earth in a pint of water, and sponge the work over with this, drying well off afterwards. In all ordinary paint a certain proportion of what is called " driers " is added to the pigments to make them dry quicker than they otherwise would. There are various forms of driers, but most of them are injurious to varnish. As turpentine is a drying liquid, no driers need be added to the last coat of paint, and thus another danger will be averted.

Red Lead should not be used under varnish, neither should barytes, whiting, or vandyke brown. These are sometimes used under varnish, either through ignorance or because of necessity. They can, however, be guarded against by those who need a specially good job. Soap and soda are sometimes used to kill grease on work which needs varnishing, but this, unless well rinsed off with clean water, is a dangerous practice. Woodwork which has been newly grained should not be varnished for some days—that is, if it has been grained in oil. If it has been

Varnishing

grained in water it may be varnished as soon as it is dry enough.

Re-varnishing.—In re-varnishing, the old varnish work must be thoroughly washed, particular care being taken to see that no dirt is left in corners or crevices. In this washing no soda should be used, or it may soften up the surface of the work and spoil the whole. Use ordinary bar soap, or a small quantity of dry soap, in hot water, but not too hot or it will soften up the varnish. Do not use flannel cloths to wash with, as the work is then left practically covered with bits from the flannel, and these show up much larger when varnished than they really are. Use only cotton cloths, such as cheese cloths or mutton cloths, which have been well washed; those of an open texture are the best for the purpose. After a good washing with the soap and water do not forget to thoroughly rinse down with clean cold water. It is not a wise plan to varnish over gilding, as the gold, being a metal, does not need the protection of the varnish, and the latter is sure to darken (sometimes blacken) the colour of the gold.

BRUSHES.

The Tools used in varnishing are not many. First of all we will take the brushes, as being the most important of the tools required by the varnisher. There are the larger brushes and the smaller ones, for broad work and narrower work respectively, and these do not differ greatly from paint brushes. They are, however, made from the very finest bristles, firmer and straighter than those used in any but the very best paint brushes. They vary from the latter in appearance in that they are generally bevelled, in consequence of their never being used upon rough preparatory work to break them into shape. Varnish brushes are also specially cemented to withstand the action of spirits; they are not always made to resist water, as they are not supposed to be put into water.

Staining and Polishing

In Fig. 41*a* will be seen the usual pattern of the large varnish brush. In Fig. 41*d* a varnish brush of more recent innovation, and one designed for highly finished woodwork and for enamels, is seen. This belongs to the flat type, of which there are many variations; but these brushes do not last so long as the other type on general work. They are, however, in a better form for leaving a high finish than

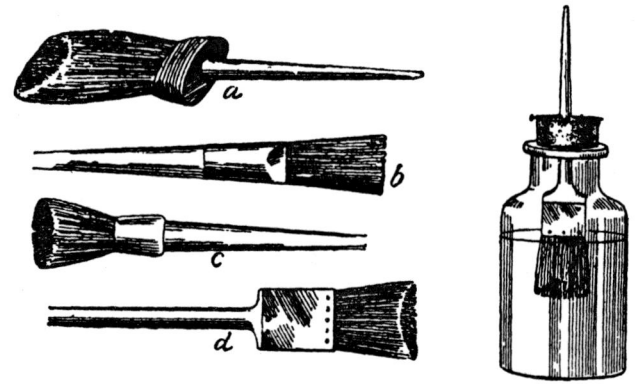

FIG. 41.—VARNISH BRUSHES.

FIG. 42.—KEEPING VARNISH BRUSHES.

the one shown in Fig. 41*a*. The tools, or smaller brushes, are shown in Fig. 41*b* and *c*. These are for use on moulds, ornamental parts, narrow bands and all small work. Some are bevelled like the larger brush, but some are not; both kinds are illustrated.

Keeping Brushes.—Paint brushes are kept in water. Varnish brushes must be kept either in linseed oil or in varnish. It is, however, recommended that for best work the brushes should be suspended in varnish. They should be kept in a clean vessel used only for that purpose, and be so suspended that the bristles are entirely covered, yet not over the head of the brush. An excellent plan for keeping varnish brushes is to procure a piece of stout wire, bore

Varnishing

a small hole through the head of the brushes, push the wire through the hole, and rest each end on the edge of the jar or the vessel containing the varnish. Fig. 42 will give some idea of what is meant. The vessel should be covered in, so as to be as airtight as possible, or the varnish inside will get thick. The cover will also keep out dust and dirt, which, if it managed to get on to the bristles of the brushes, would ruin the next job that they were used upon. Some workers keep their varnish brushes in oil, but as a certain amount of this is bound to be retained in the brush and mixed with the varnish in which the brush is next put, it is not a practice to be recommended. A spoonful of this oil would damage a canful of varnish.

Rinsing.—Before putting brushes into the varnish to be used, they should be rinsed out in a little clean turpentine, twirling the brush round to shake the turpentine back into the can or jar again. To do this properly, place the handle of the brush between both palms, and spin the brush round quickly by working each hand alternately backwards and forwards. The head of the brush should be in the can or jar whilst doing this. After this is done, place the brush as clean as possible into the work of the day, at the end of which time put it carefully away with all the precaution we have advised.

Brushes for enamelling should be kept separate from varnish brushes, but suspended in varnish in the same way, and brought into use with the same precautions. In fact you cannot possibly take too much care of brushes used for varnishing and enamelling. Novices will wash their brushes out in soap and hot water when they are finished with them for the day. This is a bad practice, however, for it is not only a very dirty job, but such washing injures the brushes. Whenever they do want washing, wash them in turpentine only. Do not on any account use a dirty brush, as that would spoil everything.

New Brushes.—For best work do not use a new brush.

Staining and Polishing

In these there are always a quantity of loose hairs which would cause much trouble.

A new brush, too, is always full of dust, which takes some time to get thoroughly rid of. It is not a bad plan to use new varnish brushes in paint for a few times, and then to thoroughly clean them out and put them into varnish.

Vessels.—The ordinary paint can is the kind of vessel most used in the trade, but there are others called patent varnish cans. The vessel which is most handy and cheapest is the ordinary earthenware pot with a side handle. Owing to smooth inner surface, and freedom from quirks caused by the joining in iron pots, it can be much more effectively cleaned than the latter kind, and as its edges are comparatively blunt there is little danger of scraping anything off the brush during the progress of the work in the event of the brush not having been cleaned thoroughly with the penknife. When such pots are not to be had, a small thin-lipped jelly mug forms an excellent substitute.

APPLYING VARNISH.

Temperature.—It is a curious fact that, generally speaking, varnishing is better done on a wet day than in warm, dry weather. On a fine morning it is usually found that objects are wet with dew, or if not very wet there is a perceptible dampness which is fatal to varnishing. On a wet day it will be noticed that there is very little or no dew deposited where the rain does not reach. This is due to the fact of the falling rain having kept the temperature uniform, and it is only when the air is quickly lowered in temperature that this moist deposit takes place. Hence it turns out that a rainy day is really the safest, so long as the work is under cover and properly ventilated. This is not well enough understood, or more perfect results would be more commonly secured.

Bloom.—The early morning is the best time of day for varnishing, because one of the chief troubles inseparable

Varnishing

from varnishing is "bloom"—a peculiar milky appearance caused chiefly by moisture collecting on the surface when the varnish is nearly dry, and remaining afterwards imprisoned in the varnish. This kind of bloom can be avoided by finishing varnishing of exposed parts early in the day, and so giving the varnish a chance to get sufficiently dry on the surface to throw off any moisture that may settle upon bright surfaces in the cool of the evening, especially after a warm day. The moisture settles on such surfaces just in the same way as the dew falls on the cool grass. The same thing applies if it is in a warm house exposed to cold air from the outside—perhaps by merely having a window left open, and so admitting a chilling draught.

It is desirable that a uniform temperature be kept in the room until the varnish is dry, because if it be too low fogging and blooming may result, while if it is too high the varnish loses in body and becomes less elastic, besides setting too quickly to allow of proper working on large surfaces. A temperature of 65° is the most suitable for the purpose. Whether the temperature be high, medium, or low, uniformity should at any rate be aimed at, for even a damp but uniform atmosphere is not after all usually detrimental to successful varnishing, whereas a sudden dampness or chilliness occurring before the work has dried may be.

Dust.—As a further aid to success there may be mentioned the need for a dustless atmosphere, although it might be said that such a condition never exists. However, precautions must be taken, and these may consist of having the floor washed, moving about with caution, and also having some clean newspaper tucked in at the bottom of the door so as to prevent the entrance of more dust. As atmospheric dust is continually falling to the floor, part of it to be raised again by currents of air or the movements of the feet, a good plan is to damp the floor with water, particularly around that portion on which the feet will stand when doing a certain piece of work.

Staining and Polishing

Dusting.—Previous to the application of varnish all the work should be thoroughly dusted. This, though a simple operation, is of the utmost importance, for upon it depends to a great extent the cleanliness of the finished work. For the best results two dusters are necessary—one for the preliminary, the other for the final, dusting. As the first dust-down is liable to make the brush dirty with dust particles, more especially when dusting objects very near the floor, it is advisable to have a second one, not only to ensure the complete removal of any trace of dust, but also to prevent dirtying the work, which is particularly necessary when dusting white or very delicately tinted work for varnishing. Needless to say, both dust brushes must be well washed in soap and water and thoroughly dried before commencing the operation, and after it has been finished sufficient time should elapse to allow any dust to settle previous to varnishing.

When about to apply Varnish, the first essential is to take the varnish bottle into the apartment where the work is to be done, for by doing this little quantities of varnish may be taken out at a time instead of having, say, a potful to begin with, which is almost sure to become dirty before it is emptied. Sufficient varnish should be put into the pot, so that the brush-tips should not touch the bottom, yet care must be taken to put in little more than will suffice for a certain part of the work. When lifting the varnish from the pot another precaution is necessary. This consists of carefully dipping the brush into the varnish, giving it a twirl so as to hold the material properly—not slapping it against the pot side, which simply causes dust, but lifting it straight on to the work. The brush should not be taken out of the pot dripping with varnish and messing the floor all over, but is so manipulated that the varnish is held in until it is put on to the work.

This having been attended to, the varnish should at once be spread with an up-and-down stroke, then crossed with a very slight pressure, and finally finished off down-

Varnishing

wards or upwards—in the one direction at any rate, an preferably the latter.

Before giving the finishing strokes, the brush should be scraped free of varnish against the edge of the pot, so that no surplus material may ooze from it when placed on the work, and so that the toe may be brought to a fine point more suited to finishing with. As varnish in itself flows to a level surface, the main point is to see that it is equally spread, for as runs are caused by more varnish being put on one place than another it follows that equal spreading is a preventative of running. Generally varnish should not be crossed more than once, or twice at the most, and the less crossed or indeed brushed at all the better. The heavier the coat the more brushing will the varnish stand, but for a perfect flow and clean finish quick finishing is essential.

The Quantity put on should vary with the number of the coats. Thus a first coat on bare wood may be full, as much as will be absorbed; other undercoatings on similar work, or on paint, should only be medium in quantity, so as to allow of proper hardening and easy glass-papering; while the last coat in every case of brush-finishing should be applied full and flowing. At the same time, too much should not be put on at the last coating, for besides increasing the risk of runs a loss of lustre may eventually occur through imperfect drying of the varnish. After work which contains moulding has been done about half an hour the mouldings should be examined, and any surplus varnish wiped out with a small tool or fitch. This is always necessary when a flowing coat has been applied, and especially with a slow-setting varnish.

FELTING DOWN.

When two or three coats of varnish are to be given, the first coats should be rubbed down smooth before the sub-

Staining and Polishing

sequent coat is put on. This may be done with powdered pumice stone, using either oil or water as a lubricant. Sometimes a shoe-brush is employed, which should be a fairly stiff bristle brush of good quality. With a painter's tools apply raw linseed oil over the varnished surface. Take up a quantity of the pumice powder on the shoe-brush and apply liberally and with plenty of friction, more oil being added if necessary. If the varnish is too hard for the pumice to cut, add a small quantity of flour emery. As the surface becomes dulled use less oil, and finish off with a drier brush and plenty of clean, soft rag, in order to leave the surface free from grease. Excess of oil, or a greasy appearance, may be corrected by wiping over with benzolene.

Very often it is desired to leave a varnished surface dull instead of the brilliant shine characteristic of varnish. The method just described is perhaps the best for such work.

The Felting Method of dulling varnished work is by using a piece of felt, or, better still, a solid felt rubber, which may be purchased ready-made. The grinding agent is pumice-stone powder of varying degrees of fineness. For the most highly finished work it is well to grind the pumice stone to avoid all extraneous grit or foreign matter which may have found its way into the powder. Stir a pound in a large basin of water, allow the coarser particles to settle, and then pour off the top water into a second basin; the finest of the powder will be in this water, and will in due time settle at the bottom, leaving the water clean.

For working, first damp the work with a sponge, using just enough good yellow soap to prevent cissing. Then soak the felt in water and sprinkle a little pumice on its face; gently rub with a light circular motion, taking large sweeps similar to the method of working French polish, and going systematically and regularly over the whole surface many times. The rubbing should be continued until a uniform dulness of surface is obtained, showing no light streaks or scratches.

Varnishing

SPIRIT VARNISHING.

The subject of spirit varnishing is of perhaps more importance to the general reader than oil varnishing. Spirit varnish is easier to make than oil varnish, and in some respects it is easier to apply, particularly on small surfaces. It is a varnish that admirably lends itself to the amateurish efforts of the beginner; but it is also a varnish capable of producing a very high-class finish if placed in practised hands. Its manner of application is very different from that of oil varnish, for whilst the latter is slow-drying spirit varnish is very quick-drying. Owing to the fact that it dries so quickly, caused by the spirits evaporating, it is not suitable for large plain surfaces.

The object in varnishing is not only to produce a gloss, but also to produce an absolutely smooth surface. This object is not attained when the joinings overlap each other and create ridges. There is, however, at least one advantage that spirit varnish possesses over oil varnish, and this lies in the comparatively easy way in which the varnish can be rubbed down smooth. A small quantity of naphtha or methylated spirit on a wad of cotton wadding will soon remove any ridges or uneven places on the surface of the varnish, provided it has not been allowed to get too hard and dry.

The successful spirit varnisher should have a knowledge of French polishing. Unlike oil varnish, spirit varnish does not flow level after leaving the brush, and here lies the chief difficulty in applying it. Each successive coat should be levelled with either very fine glass-paper or the polish rubber, and success will be more certain if before any varnish is applied the pores of the wood are sealed with either size or French polish. This will prevent the unequal absorption of the varnish, and if polish is used instead of size the grain will not rise as much as when an aqueous solution such as size is applied over it.

Staining and Polishing

Brushes for applying Spirit Varnish should preferably be small ones, and those known in the trade as camel-hair will be quite suitable. Brushes bound in tin should be avoided, as the shellac in the varnish will corrode the tin. The latter will then react upon the varnish, and turn it dark-coloured. The vessel used to hold the varnish should be an earthenware or glass jar, and absolutely clean.

Applying.—As regards the mode of application much depends upon the nature of the articles being varnished. The inexperienced almost invariably apply too much varnish, with the inevitable result that the work cracks. It should be laid on in the same direction as the grain of the wood, as evenly and regularly as possible. The manner of applying resembles that of staining, particularly the water- and spirit-stains, and we cannot do better than direct the reader's attention to the chapter dealing with the application of stains (page 15). In panelled work the panels should be done first, then the stiles, and finally the mouldings. (See Fig. 1, page 16.)

The varnish should be rubbed down between every coat, so as to keep the work smooth as it proceeds. Care should be exercised in the rubbing, lest the edges or prominent members of moulding be rubbed too much, which will make the subsequent coats sink in at such places and render the finished surface uneven in gloss. The last application of varnish will be better if at the close of the rubbing-down process (which should be done with about half spirits and half polish) a few drops of glaze are added to the rubber.

Many spirit enamels are simply spirit varnish with an addition of dry colour of the necessary shade. These enamels should be applied and got up in much the same manner as ordinary spirit varnish.

For Small Fretted Articles spirit varnish is much to be preferred to oil varnish, owing to its thinner body and intense hardness and quickness in drying. All edges should

Varnishing

be done first, and end-grains should have one or two extra coats to bring such parts up to the level of the rest of the work. It may be mentioned here that in either polishing or varnishing thin fretwork, both sides of the wood should be coated, as this not only shows a better finish, but incidentally acts as a preservative, and also prevents the wood from warping. (See also FRETWORK POLISHING, page 123.)

VARNISHING FLOOR MARGINS.

A job which often falls to the lot of the practical man is the margin on the floor of a sitting-room between the edge of the carpet square and the skirting board, and a few hints on its treatment will be of service. After well scrubbing, size the parts to be stained with glue-size as used by painters. The application of size is to stop the suction, or prevent the excess absorption of the stain, as otherwise, on such comparatively coarse surfaces as flooring-boards, some places being more spongy would be darker than others.

When this is quite dry, rub lightly with No. 1 glass-paper and dust well off, when it is ready for the stain. This is made by mixing the required colour pigment in equal quantities of varnish, linseed oil and turpentine; strain before use. When this coat is dry and quite hard (better for standing a day or two), go over again with fine glass-paper, stop up all nail holes and joints with stained putty, and wipe over with a damp wash-leather before varnishing.

If a more durable job is desired, two coats of varnish should be given, adding a small quantity of turps to the first, which should be well brushed out; the final coat of varnish should be generously used and well worked in all directions. Use a good *hard*-drying varnish, such as church oak, or floor varnish.

For oil-polishing floors, see page 136, and for wax-polishing floors, page 141.

Staining and Polishing

OUTDOOR POLISHED AND VARNISHED WORK.

During the last few years wheelwrights, coach and railway carriage builders and tramcar makers have with advantage bodied up much of their work, such as panels, etc., with French polish. After this treatment they are coated with the best pale carriage varnish, owing to the fact that ordinary polish will not stand the weather. Many shop fronts are now treated in this manner. The timber is filled in, bodied up, coloured, and fastened, after which a good outside varnish is used to finish up the work. This prevents the unsightly bare patches so often seen on outside work when only polish has been used.

FLATTING VARNISH.

This is a varnish that really belongs to the class of spirit varnishes, and is one that dries quickly, but without gloss. It produces what is termed a flat or matt finish, which gives a very rich appearance to some woods, particularly the darker varieties. Flatting varnish may be made by adding white wax to ordinary copal varnish, and thinning out with turpentine. Both the varnish and the wax should be heated for this purpose, and also the turpentine should be warmed a little before adding to the varnish. Heating the several ingredients assists in the amalgamation.

This varnish is applied in the same manner as ordinary spirit varnish, as it dries quickly. It is, however, usually done upon a full-gloss oil varnish, and thus requires expert handling in order to avoid bright flashes or patches, caused by not properly covering up the glossy surface underneath. Should the edges of the varnish be allowed to set before joining up, such parts will look partially bright when dry. The varnish is a thin one, and is consequently easily applied. With practice it may be laid upon the work with much speed, which it requires.

FAULTS IN VARNISHING AND THEIR REMEDIES

Common Faults—General Hints on Varnishing.

BLOOM.—Perhaps the most prevalent of defects in varnishing is what has already been termed "bloom" (page 166). The varnish takes on a whitish film or sort of mist, which may come and go, or may remain permanent. The defect is more common among the better class of varnishes than among the cheaper ones. The smooth, glossy surface offered to the air by good varnish induces the condensation upon it of the moisture in the atmosphere. If this takes place before the varnish is thoroughly hard, bloom is certain to result. It is, however, sometimes caused by water in the varnish—that is, moisture in the gum from which it is made, and which has not been properly eliminated. Vapour arising from a damp floor is also liable to cause blooming. Varnish which has been left uncorked for some time, or which has been stored in some damp place, will also bloom.

To avoid Blooming the work must be freely ventilated (but without draughts), so as to hasten the drying as far as possible. An even temperature should also, if at all possible, be kept in the room where the varnishing is taking place. Blooming due to moisture or frost may be removed by warmth, washing and brisk rubbing with warm water, or rubbing with a wad and olive oil. It is sometimes cured by rubbing with oil and vinegar, afterwards wiping quite dry. But when it is due to the varnish itself, it can seldom be entirely eradicated without re-varnishing. In some cases it may be necessary to clean the varnish right off before revarnishing, and this might be done with ammonia.

Dead or Sleepy Patches.—These terms imply that the varnish is lacking its full lustre in certain places. The

Staining and Polishing

causes may be unseasoned timber, soft undercoats, or through the ground being very porous, and abnormal suction taking place. An unequal distribution of the varnish will cause the same defects, for where it is barely applied there will naturally be less gloss than where it is freely applied. Another good coat of varnish is necessary as a remedy.

Blistering.—The varnish rising in places like blisters is caused by heat playing on the surface and softening the undercoats; or when moisture is imprisoned underneath the varnish, the heat on the surface causes the water to form into vapour, and this, expanding, lifts the varnish. To remedy, clean off and re-varnish.

Cracking.—This is produced by using a hard varnish over an elastic one, or by coating over paint which is only partly dry. The soft undercoats expand and contract with the varying temperatures, and so pull apart in places the upper hard varnish, which does not respond to the same influences. Diluting the varnish with too much turpentine will also cause cracking. If not too badly cracked, it may be remedied by rubbing down and giving another coat of varnish. Cracking often occurs on varnished bakers' vans, owing to hot bread being placed inside the van.

Pinholing and Cissing.—These are caused by a recession of the varnish from a given point, usually a grease spot or a minute hole. This must be provided against by thorough rubbing down and wash-leathering before varnishing.

Pock Marks or Pitting.—These are marks or indentations which do not extend to the ground (as in cissing), but are in the varnish itself. They are caused by the presence of steam or smoke or hot moist air in the room when the varnish is applied. They may also be caused by turps in the varnish brush. These marks can only be removed by rubbing down and re-varnishing.

Faults in Varnishing and their Remedies

Flaking and Peeling.—This consists in portions of the varnish separating from the ground. These faults are not very frequent, but when they do occur it is very probable that they are caused by a lack of cohesion between the different coats of varnish, or between the varnish and ground, or by the undercoats being greasy, or by drying too hard. Or they may be caused by moisture in the wood by poor vehicles, or by bad pigments.

Grittiness.—This is sometimes caused in the varnish by its being stored in a cold, damp atmosphere, by frost upon the cans during transit, or by chill to the varnish. Sometimes the fault lies in using a varnish of a too new manufacture. Dirty brushes and dirty methods of working are all too prevalent causes of grittiness.

Specks.—These are formed in varnish by similar conditions. No cure is possible other than grinding down and re-varnishing.

Perishing, or Gradual Loss of Lustre.—These troubles are invariably caused by too frequent washing with hot water, or from the influence of damp, ammonia, coal gas, salt sea air, or limestone.

Wrinkles or Crinking.—This defect occurs from too heavy a coat of varnish, or when it has not been sufficiently brushed out.

Creeping.—This is a similar defect, the result of similar causes. It is also caused by the presence of oily patches on the groundwork, or by varnishing in too low a temperature. As the result is an uneven surface, the varnish should be cleaned off, after being rubbed down smooth with pumice stone and water.

Streakiness in the varnish may be caused by the imperfect mixing of driers, oil, or turpentine with the varnish. When it appears on unpainted wood, it may be due to uneven planing or filling-up. Very often an extra coat of varnish will put the thing right.

Staining and Polishing

Varnish not Drying.—Much of the cheap, poor quality varnish possesses this particular defect. In the use of good varnishes it will very rarely occur, unless there has been some fault in the preparation of the surface or in the manner of applying. Varnish will not dry on a greasy surface. When it is desired to varnish some old work which is probably greasy, an application of weak lime laid over the greasy parts, allowed to dry and then brushed off, will kill the grease. A solution of common washing soda or benzolene will also suffice. Neglect of these precautions (the use of a brush that is not perfectly clean, or of a brush that has been suspended in oil and the oil not eradicated, the use of varnish that has been left uncorked or otherwise exposed to atmospheric influences for a long period) will prevent oil varnish from drying properly.

Varnish that remains quite wet on the article in hand should be cleaned off with turpentine and cotton rag. On no account should flannel or other woollen cloths be used for this purpose. If the varnish is merely tacky—that is, sticky to the touch, but not properly wet—then a coat of terebine (liquid drier) should be given to the work, and afterwards another coat of varnish.

Ropey Surface.—Much apparently unexplainable trouble arises from the fact that varnish is thoughtlessly exposed to different temperatures before use. Varnish is certain to turn out "ropey" and "curdling" when it has been standing for some time in a cold, damp place, and has been brought straight into a warm room and used. On the other hand, it will look poor and thin if brought out of a hot, stuffy place and used straight away on a cold job, such as outside on a cold or damp day.

Finger-marks may sometimes be removed from varnished work by saturating a piece of chamois leather with sweet oil and applying it gently to them.

Dull Varnished Surfaces can often be brightened by

Faults in Varnishing and their Remedies

washing with clean cold water or a mixture of equal parts of vinegar, turpentine, and raw linseed oil, and finally polishing with a piece of chamois leather or soft flannel. Another mixture consists of 1 gill of spirits, 1 pint of raw linseed oil, 1 gill of vinegar, and 1 oz. of butter of antimony. This must be applied very quickly. A vigorous rubbing with a wash-leather is, however, a more desirable means of heightening the lustre of varnish than the use of the above mixtures, as there is then no fear of any ill after-effects, such as the cracking of the varnish, which may occur as a result of a too liberal use of these mixtures or by employing inferior materials.

TESTING VARNISHES.

Varnishes may be tested by spreading them upon a piece of plate glass, and by using them upon a flat, white painted ground, or a white piece of wood well sized to prevent absorption. The former method is the test for hardness, drying and tenacity; the latter for colour, fineness, body and flow. One of the good qualities of varnish is that it should dry throughout, and not merely skin over hard on the surface. This may be tested by using the varnish as if it were gold-size, putting it on rather freely, and as soon as tacky gilding it. If it is a varnish that dries superficially first, it will cause the gold to wrinkle in a few hours, and the greater this wrinkling the more faulty the varnish is in this respect. This is, however, by no means the most important point to consider in a good varnish, as some of the best have this fault, especially finishing varnishes. A method of testing the elasticity of a varnish is to apply two coats of it on a piece of tin, and when dry to bend the tin; or coat a sheet of parchment paper or linen, and after it has properly dried try its flexibility or tendency to chip off by crumpling the material between the hands.

Staining and Polishing

GENERAL HINTS ON VARNISHING.

In applying varnish to the work the following points must be attended to. Flow on a good body of varnish, and do not rub it out barely; rather put on as much as you can without allowing it to run.

Uniformity.—Be careful to lay it equally over the whole surface, not thinner in one part than another. Do not allow it to accumulate in corners, crevices, quirks, or mouldings, and all such places where it will gather and wrinkle, even if it does not flow out over the adjoining piece of plain surface and produce unsightly runs. Do not work it about unnecessarily; it must not be crossed and re-crossed, but judgment must be used to place it exactly where required straight away, without any unnecessary after-spreading.

Undercoats.—When giving undercoats of varnish which are to be rubbed down, it is best to use less than for a finishing coat, as if the coat be a thick heavy one it will take too long to harden sufficiently to rub down with safety and certainty. The edges of the wet varnish must not be allowed to set before attempting to join on with another patch, but must be kept well alive. A perfect job of varnishing cannot be produced with less than three coats, of which the first must be well felted down with pumice stone.

Mixtures.—Do not mix varnishes of different makes, unless it is known by experience what the result will be. There is no danger, however, in mixing two varnishes of a similar class; for instance, flatting varnish may be mixed with copal varnish (full gloss) to obtain medium or egg-shell gloss. Japan black may be mixed with copal varnish to obtain a thin transparent stained varnish. Many other mixtures are both desirable and useful. But ordinary spirit varnishes should never be mixed with oil varnishes or lacquers. Free turpentine or raw linseed oil should not be added to varnish.

Light is necessary to the proper hardening of varnish,

Faults in Varnishing and their Remedies

as well as air. After newly-varnished work is dry it may be hardened somewhat by well sousing it with clean cold water; the water contains a high percentage of oxygen, which is given out to the varnish.

Double-Coating.—In ordinary practice it is sometimes useful to double-coat work instead of felting down and re-varnishing. A very fine gloss can be got in this way. Give the work a medium coat of varnish, and when this is tacky (not dry) repeat a coat of the same varnish, working very lightly and rapidly, taking care not to work up the undercoating. Great care and skill are required to do this perfectly, as the less hard the undercoat is the finer will the gloss and finish be. No preparation of any kind must be used between the two coats.

In Selecting Varnishes for various kinds of work, care and experience are necessary. In work intended to be felted down, a good quality hard oil varnish is desirable; quick hard varnishes rub up chalky, and scratch readily. The paleness of a varnish is not always a criterion of its value, and the palest varnishes are not the best for general work. For light work, of course, they are necessary on account of their paleness.

Straining.—Varnish ought not to require straining, but if by reason of accidental agitation or other cause it does require it, the straining is best accomplished by lightly plugging a wide-nosed funnel with about an inch and a half of cotton wadding, and tying a bit of coarse muslin over the nozzle to keep it in; the varnish is then allowed to trickle through of its own weight. A fine cambric or linen handkerchief makes a fairly good strainer, if the varnish is allowed to find its way through without any stirring or forcing.

OAK CABINET WITH SHAPED BACK, SUITABLE FOR FUMED AND WAX-POLISHED FINISH.

APPENDIX

RECIPES FOR STAINS, POLISHES, FILLERS, ETC.

As many workers prefer to make up the stains and polishes, etc., which they may require, instructions are here given for making stains which will yield an exact imitation of the different woods named. The wood to be stained should of course be white, or very light in colour.

MAHOGANY STAINS.

Chemical Stain.—For real mahogany or baywood:—
Bichromate of potash dissolved in water.
Bichromate of potash and liquid ammonia and water give a very dark stain.

Water Stains.—For light-coloured woods such as pine, birch, etc., mix burnt sienna in stale beer and water, equal parts; then use coloured polish or varnish. Burnt sienna in water mixed with a little glue size as a binder is excellent for staining.

MAHOGANY STAINS FOR AMERICAN WHITEWOOD

Oil Stain.—Venetian red mixed with raw linseed oil, with a little drier, used thin.

Spirit Stain.—Dissolve 2 ozs. of orange shellac in 1 pint of methylated spirit, and add sufficient bismarck brown or red sander's wood until the desired depth is obtained. Strain before using.

Chemical Stain.—See above: Stains for real mahogany or baywood.

SHERATON MAHOGANY.

Chemical Stain.—Stain real mahogany or baywood with a weak solution of bichromate of potash; if not dark enough, add a little liquid ammonia to the solution; when dry use red oil. Or fume the mahogany with ammonia and use red oil.

Appendix

CHIPPENDALE MAHOGANY.

Chemical Stain.—Use a heavy walnut stain on American whitewood, satin walnut, or other light-coloured wood; fill in, and then body up with red polish, or stain with shoemaker's ink, obtainable at any leather grindery warehouse; fill in, and body up with red polish.

WALNUT STAINS.

Water Stain.—Mix vandyke brown, or equal parts vandyke brown and burnt umber, into a thin paste with liquid ammonia. Thin down to required tone with water.

Oil Stain.—Brunswick black thinned with turpentine until the proper shades are obtained. Add a little varnish to improve it.

Spirit Stain.—¼ lb. asphaltum dissolved in 1 pint of naphtha. Useful for common work.

Chemical Stain.—1 oz. Epsom salts, 1 oz. permanganate of potash, dissolved separately in 1 pint each of boiling water, and mixed together and applied hot with a fibre (not bristle) brush or a sponge.

OAK STAINS.

Water Stain.—Mix ¼ lb. vandyke brown and ¼ pint of ammonia with water, or liquid ammonia diluted with water.

Oil Stain.—¼ lb. crushed asphaltum dissolved in 1 pint of turpentine.

Spirit Stain.—2 ozs. vandyke brown in oil; ¼ pint of turpentine; ¼ pint of kerosine or paraffin oil. If too dark add more paraffin. Stain may be brightened by using a little raw sienna (in oil) instead of all vandyke.

Chemical Stain.—Mix 2 ozs. of pearlash and 2 ozs. of American potash in 1 quart of hot water.

Solution of bichromate of potash for dark golden oak.

ROSEWOOD STAINS.

Water Stain.—Logwood, one part; water, ten parts. Apply warm. Vary the applications upon the surface to get effect.

Oil Stain.—Venetian red; a small proportion of black; mix in linseed oil to which has been added a little terebine.

Appendix

Spirit Stain.—First coat with mahogany spirit stain; the figure can then be put in with a sponge or feather dipped in black polish.

Chemical Stain.—A solution of permanganate of potash. Strong solution of bichromate of potash on mahogany, coloured up to obtain the wavy dark grain.

EBONY STAINS.

Water Stain.—1 lb. of logwood chips, cut fine; ¼ lb. of brazilwood, cut fine, in 1½ gallons of clean rainwater. This is used as a first coating while hot. Before this is dry apply a second solution made up of ¼ lb. gall nuts dissolved in 1 gallon of water. Two or three coats will give a colour sufficiently dense. Finally, go over the whole with a solution of sulphate of iron, consisting of 1 quart of water and 2 ozs. iron.

Oil Stain.—Ordinary drop black with driers in boiled linseed oil.

Spirit Stain.—Spirit black thinned with japanner's gold size and turpentine.

Chemical Stain.—Mix 1 lb. logwood, 3 pints of water, 1 oz. pearlash, and apply hot; next apply another solution composed of a quart of water, ½ oz. verdigris, ¼ oz. green copperas, to which is added a handful of iron filings in 1 pint of hot vinegar.

Shoemaker's ink is one of the simplest of stains for this purpose.

MAPLE AND SATINWOOD STAINS.

Water Stain.—Grind raw sienna in clear water, and add a little burnt sienna. If too dark add a little whiting.

Oil Stain.—Take above colours, but ground in oil, with a drop of terebine.

Spirit Stain.—1¼ quart of methylated spirits; 1½ ozs. of gamboge; 3 ozs. ground turmeric.

Chemical Stain.—Applications of nitric acid or sulphate of iron.

Weak solution of bichromate of potash makes a good satinwood stain.

Appendix

CHERRYWOOD STAINS.

Water Stain.—Take dark yellow ochre and dissolve well in water; add a little stale beer to fasten the colour, and apply one coat. When dry coat with best red lake.

Oil Stain.—Mix together 1 quart of spirits of turpentine, 1 pint of varnish, 1 lb. dry burnt sienna. After it has been on five minutes wipe off with rags.

Spirit Stain.—Digest red sander's wood in spirits of wine, and thin with methylated spirits to shade.

Chemical Stain.—Dissolve 3 ozs. of bismarck brown in 1 gallon boiling water. Add 1 gill of vinegar to set the colour and prevent fading. When cold it is ready for use.

WATER COATING.

We here give a few recipes under the class of staining designated as "water coating." The colours used are dry colours, ground up in water, and prepared for use in size:—

Mahogany.—Venetian red, ochre, and mahogany lake.

Rosewood.—Mahogany lake, rose pink, and lamp black.

Oak.—Burnt umber and ochre.

Ebony.—Ivory black.

Satinwood or Maple.—Yellow ochre and chrome.

Walnut.—Burnt umber and Venetian red.

Cherry.—Mahogany lake and yellow ochre.

Apply these while the size is in solution, and wipe down with a dusting brush, leaving streaky marks. When dry, size and varnish. This process is useful for temporary work or cheap furniture.

SELF-COLOURS.

Very often self-colours are desired, irrespective of imitating any particular wood, especially in imitating intarsia or marquetry work. Hence the following:—

Blue (Water).—Add 1 lb. indigo, 2 lbs. woad, and 3 ozs. alum in 1 gallon of boiling water, and apply hot.

Blue (Oil).—Prussian blue in oil.

Blue (Chemical).—Dissolve indigo in dilute sulphuric acid, adding a little whiting to modify.

Appendix

Brown (Water).—¼ lb. vandyke brown, 1d. burnt sienna, and 1 lb. washing soda. Add 2 quarts of water, and boil for twenty minutes.

Brown (Oil).—3 parts Indian red; 2 parts lamp black; 1 part ochre.

Brown (Spirit).—4 ozs. dragon's blood, 1 oz. soda to 3 pints spirits of wine.

Brown (Chemical).—Hold wood to fire, and when warm apply nitric acid with a brush until a fine brown is obtained.

Chocolate (Water).—Burnt sienna and vandyke brown in water.

Chocolate (Oil).—Indian red, lamp black, ochre, and vermilion.

Chocolate (Spirit).—1 lb. madder; 2 ozs. common soda; 8 ozs. fustic; 10 ozs. dragon's blood. Dissolve in 6 pints methylated spirits.

Crimson (Water).—Boil 1 lb. brazilwood in 3 pints of water for an hour; then add ¼ oz. cochineal. Boil again for half an hour, when it is ready for use.

Crimson (Oil).—Crimson lake in oil.

Green (Water).—Yellow arsenic and indigo in water.

Green (Oil).—Prussian blue and raw sienna.

Green (Spirit).—Indigo and turmeric dissolved in spirit.

Green (Chemical).—Hot solution of verdigris in vinegar.

Grey (Oil).—Whiting, French ochre, raw sienna, and lamp black.

Grey (Chemical).—A solution of blue copperas in water or vinegar.

Orange (Water).—Mahogany lake, raw sienna, and chrome yellow.

Orange (Oil).—Orange chrome.

Orange (Spirit).—1 oz. powdered turmeric in 6 ozs. spirits of wine.

Purple (Water).—Logwood and brazilwood solution, to which gall must be added. Finally, use a pearlash solution to obtain the desired tint.

Purple (Oil).—Indian red, whiting, and ultramarine.

Purple (Spirit).—Dissolve ½ lb. madder, ¼ lb. fustic, ¼ lb. dragon's blood, and 1 oz. common soda in 3 pints of spirits.

Appendix

Red (Water).—1 lb. brazilwood, 1 oz. pearlash, and apply hot. Then add a solution of 1½ ozs. of alum to 1 quart of water to the surface already treated as above.

Red (Oil).—Crimson lake or vermilion.

Red (Spirit).—Macerate red sander's wood in rectified spirits of naphtha.

Red (Chemical).—Archil dye, slightly diluted, applied warm, finally passing over the work with a pearlash solution.

Scarlet (Oil).—Vermilion or vermilionette.

Scarlet (Spirit).—Macerate red sander's wood in rectified naphtha until required shade is obtained.

Yellow (Water).—Yellow ochre or lemon chrome mixed with size and applied warm. Wipe surplus off with rag.

Yellow (Oil).—Yellow ochre or lemon chrome, according to shade required.

Yellow (Spirit).—1 oz. turmeric in 1 pint of methylated spirits. Colour can be varied by altering strength.

Yellow (Chemical).—Dilute ½ oz. nitric acid with 1½ ozs. distilled water; if too dark add more water.

ANILINE DYES.

These dyes can be obtained from practically all druggists and are sold by the ounce. They are in powder form and are of two kinds—one dissolving in water, the other in spirits. To the former a little vinegar must be added to bind or fasten the colour to the work. They can be procured in almost any colour, and may be usefully employed on wood for self-colours, as well as for imitating various woods.

RECIPES FOR POLISHES, ETC.

It will be found that materials of the first quality always answer best. The old rule for each workman to mix his own materials is almost out of date, as all requisites can now be obtained from firms who make their preparations a speciality, and these are, on the whole, of a uniform character. As, however, it is sometimes a convenience to be able to prepare the materials—and, moreover, it is a good principle for workers to know what they consist of—the following list of materials and modes of preparation may be found useful.

Appendix

Now-a-days it is, perhaps, hardly worth the trouble entailed to make one's own polish, for, whilst the home-made article may carry with it an assurance as to quality of ingredients, the manufactures of well-known firms can be usually relied upon for quality. Although in all probability, however, the worker will prefer to buy his materials ready mixed, the following particulars will help him to understand the nature of the various polishes.

French Polish.—This is a comprehensive term applied to each or any of the undermentioned polishes, though these latter have certain distinctions which specially fit them for certain classes of work. Generally speaking, what is usually termed French polish is made from the yellow flake shellac, though sometimes other gums are added, such as sandarac, tragacanth, gum juniperi, mastic, etc., in order to give a better lustre to the finished work. From 4 ozs. to 5 ozs. of flake shellac dissolved in 1 pint of methylated spirit will make a good French polish. (See page 39 for Shellac.)

Another recipe for a useful French polish is 2 ozs. button lac and 3 ozs. orange shellac to 1 pint of spirit.

To stain French polish red, mix 4 ozs. of red sander's or 1 oz. of bismarck brown and 1 pint of methylated spirit; strain through fine muslin, and use with the yellow polish as required.

Button Polish.—Button polish is very similar to French polish, but rather paler, and also a little dearer. It is made from button shellac, and is yellowish-brown in colour. It is mostly used for the yellow woods, and also for the darker ones. Mix 5 ozs. of button shellac with 1 pint of methylated spirit; stir constantly to prevent the lac (which should be broken up into small pieces) from sticking together.

Garnet Polish.—Garnet polish is made from garnet shellac, as its name implies. It is more transparent than either French polish or button polish, although a trifle darker. It is a very useful polish for rich dark woods, such as mahogany, walnut, and rosewood, or for darkening any wood where purity of tone is required. Ingredients: 5 ozs. garnet shellac to 1 pint of methylated spirit.

Dark Polish.—Rather cheaper in price than lighter-coloured goods, but equally good in effect, and is useful for woods of dark colour, such as black walnut, dark oak, mahogany, etc. Its ingredients vary with the different makes, but it often contains button, orange, and garnet lacs. 5 ozs. of the lac should be used to 1 pint of spirit.

Appendix

White Polish.—Where purity of tone is required this is perhaps the best polish, especially for very light woods and for inlay and transfer work. It is made from white or bleached shellac; that is, ordinary shellac from which the colour has been extracted. Mix 4 ozs. or 5 ozs. of broken white shellac with 1 pint of spirit; spread out to dry before mixing; shake occasionally until dissolved, and strain through coarse muslin.

To stain white polish for ebonising, mix 1 oz. of gas-black or drop-black and $\frac{1}{4}$ oz. of finely ground Prussian blue and $\frac{1}{2}$ pint of methylated spirit, and use with white polish as required.

Transparent Polish.—This polish is used for work similar to that for which the last-mentioned polish is employed. It is made from bleached shellac, and is quite clear and transparent. It is used where exceptionally light tones are required, and although it is not so lasting as that made from darker lacs, it works up to a very brilliant finish. Unless carefully worked, it is liable to become tacky, and it also has a tendency to crack with age.

Orange or Brown Polish.—Very similar to the ordinary French polish. Made from orange shellac, a brown flaky gum, it is used on any but very light woods, and can be stained if required. Ingredients: Methylated spirit, 1 pint; orange shellac, 6 ozs. Shake the mixture at intervals to assist the lac to dissolve.

Brush Polish.—Brush polish is a common variety used for fatting or bodying in, and is applied to the work with a camel-hair brush or mop. To make it, increase the quantity of gums given in the recipes for polish by 25 per cent. Commercial brush polish is not usually of as fine a quality as French polish, and is used for filling up the grain as a substitute for a mixture of French polish and spirit varnish.

Glaze.—Known in the trade as glace, "slick," "guish," "lightning," slake, and telegraph. This is made from gum benzoin and methylated spirit. Its composition and use have been fully explained on p. 77. It is made from gum benzoin, and is used for quickly imparting a lustre to polished work upon which it is not desired to spend the time necessary for spiriting the work out. It is particularly useful in dealing with carved and open work, where it is difficult to manipulate the rubber. Glaze improves with age and, therefore, should not be made for immediate use. Its ingredients are 6 ozs. gum benzoin to 1 pint of methylated spirit. When selecting gum

Appendix

benzoin obtain that containing a high percentage of white matter, as it is the best quality.

NOTE.—All these polishes should be made in the proportion of 4 ozs., 5 ozs., or 6 ozs. of shellac or gum to 1 pint of methylated spirit.

Colouring.—In cases where it is desired to darken the colours of woods without previous staining, the use of coloured polish is often resorted to. All polishes, with the exception of white and colourless, have a slightly darkening effect on the wood, and in adding stains to the polish this should be borne in mind. Red and black polishes can be obtained ready-made, but the most usual means of colouring is by the addition of spirit stains. These are also obtainable ready mixed for use, although they can be easily mixed up by the worker, directions for which have already been given.

Dry powders should never be added direct to the polish, but should be previously dissolved in methylated spirit and the liquid strained in order that the polish may be free from particles of grit.

Gums.—Besides the ordinary commercial polishes, some polishers consider that certain gums added to the polish have particularly good effects, and for this reason the following gums are often added by the polishers, either together or separately, to attain the desired results, viz., benzoin, $\frac{1}{4}$ oz. to 1 pint; sandarac, $\frac{1}{2}$ oz. to 1 pint; elemi resin, $\frac{1}{4}$ oz. to 1 pint; mastic, $\frac{1}{2}$ oz. to 1 pint; gum-thus and tragacanth, $\frac{1}{4}$ oz. to 1 pint. Whether or not the addition of one or more of these gums proves beneficial must be judged from experience, as different materials yield various results, according to the worker handling them.

A little gum copal dissolved in 90 per cent. alcohol, or pure spirit, is added to the polish to give a harder surface. (Gum copal will not dissolve in methylated spirit.) The addition of gum copal is a safeguard against sweating.

Methylated Spirit (spirit of wine to which is added a certain quantity of mineral naphtha and other adulterants).—The spirit used for polishing should be pure, and the strength about 65° over-proof. Hence Continental polishers who are allowed to use a pure spirit have an advantage. Care should be taken in buying methylated spirit that it is not the compound known as "methylated finish," which contains a large percentage of resin—an undesirable addition, especially in finishing off work. The reason for the presence of resin in the

Appendix

spirit is that, provided it contains a certain percentage of foreign matter, no licence is necessary for its sale. Unless the worker buys his spirit in sufficiently large quantities to warrant his dealing with a wholesale house for it, he will do well to deal with a local chemist, who will supply the pure stuff at the same price as it can be obtained from a retail oil and colour merchant, and thus do away with the risk of purchasing an inferior article which might spoil otherwise good work.

Oils.—The oils used for polishing are linseed, poppy, and almond oils, and of the three the first-named is the one most commonly met with. In polishing, it is generally considered that the less oil used the better, its presence only being required, as far as the actual work is concerned, to assist the rubber in running over the surface of the work. In the preliminary stages of the work it is customary to wipe the wood over with oil and allow it to stand for an hour or so in order that the figure may be brought out and the beauty enhanced. For oiling mahogany, red oil should be used, this being made by steeping 2 ozs. of alkanet root in 1 pint of linseed oil. When the oil has become sufficiently coloured, it should be strained through fine muslin.

Floor Polish.—Many people who admire polished floors are debarred from having them by considerations of cost and upkeep, but an ordinary deal floor filled and stained by one or other of the methods described and regularly wax-polished (after a preliminary coat of floor varnish) will be a source of joy to its owner, to say nothing of its sanitary advantages. The most suitable polish for this purpose is one which has made great strides into favour of late years—the well-known ronuk. It is a wax polish ready compounded, which is supplied in tins of various sizes for those who only require small quantities and in bulk for use in large houses and public buildings. It will rapidly produce a high gloss on polished woodwork, having at the same time a cleansing effect, and where a large quantity of polishing has to be done it is a great saver of time and labour.

Ronuk is also of great use for carved work and renovating old furniture, besides being serviceable for other purposes outside the scope of this handbook. It can be applied with a rubber or brush, no special skill being required for its use, and for floor work in large institutions the makers supply special rubbers and brushes.

Johnson's prepared wax is one of the best for oak furniture and reviving motor car body work.

Appendix

FURNITURE REVIVERS.

Furniture polish revivers are generally used after the work has been washed down so as to remove the dirt, etc. If work shows any signs of sweating a reviver is used to freshen up the polish. Make a wad or rubber of cotton wadding, and well moisten it with the reviver; use the rubber in a similar manner as when french polishing, and then dry off and well polish with a warm dry duster.

Recipe for Furniture Reviver.—1 gill vinegar, 1 gill methylated spirit, ¼ pint raw linseed oil, and 1 oz. butter of antimony.

Some workers add a piece of camphor the size of a thimble.

Furniture revivers should be used with care, because the action of a reviver is to partially re-dissolve the gums used in the original polishing process.

There are many revivers offered to the public by the wholesale houses; one of the best is that made and patented by T. E. Lambert.

FILLERS.

The following recipes for fillers for various woods may be taken as suggestions. The proportions given will of course be determined by individual requirements.

Ash.—This being a very light wood, it requires a filler with no colour added. It is also a very open-pored wood. Mix together two parts of pale linseed oil, three parts of pale japan gold-size, and one part of turpentine; then add floated silica to form a paste. Thin for use with turpentine.

Beech and Birch.—Coat with white or bleached shellac in the proportion of ½ lb. shellac to ½ gallon of spirit.

Cherry is a close-grained wood and requires coating with shellac as for beech. For a filler, mix in the proportion of—best whiting, 5 lbs.; plaster-of-paris, 2 lbs.; burnt sienna, dry, 1½ ozs.; venetian red, dry, 1 oz.; boiled oil, 1 quart; turpentine, 1 pint; brown japan, 1 pint. Silica may be used in place of the whiting and plaster.

Chestnut is a very coarse-grained wood, and the filler needs to be rather stiff. Use plain silica filler, either slightly stained to match colour of wood or not.

Ebony.—Make a filler with plaster-of-paris and lamp black, mixed to a paste with either japan or gold-size.

Appendix

Elm requires the same filler as chestnut.

Mahogany.—Take equal parts by weight of whiting, plaster-of-paris, fine pumice powder, and litharge, to which may be added a little soap-stone and vandyke brown, ochre, or burnt sienna. Mix, then make to a paste with 1 pint of japan, 2 pints of boiled oil, and 3 pints of turpentine, and grind down.

Maple.—Coat or fill with white shellac varnish.

Oak.—In the proportion of—whiting, 5 lbs.; plaster-of-paris, 2 lbs.; dry burnt sienna, ½ oz.; raw linseed oil, 1 quart; turpentine, 1 pint; white shellac, ½ pint. Mix together. Or mix together two parts of turpentine, one part of raw oil, and sufficient japan to dry the filler in the usual time; add to this liquid fine silica to form a paste. Or mix equal parts by weight of raw oil, japan gold-size, and turpentine. Add burnt umber in oil, or vandyke brown with a little drop-black in oil, to colour the mass.

Oak (Dark).—The filler for ebony will do also for dark oak, or burnt umber may be used in place of lamp black.

Oak (Golden).—Take in the proportion of 5 lbs. good uncoloured paste filler, 2 ozs. of burnt umber and ¼ pint of best asphaltum varnish. Mix to a paste.

Pine.—Coat with bleached shellac varnish. Cheap work is generally given a coat of clear size and rubbed down before applying the shellac varnish.

Satin Walnut.—Adopt the same method as for beech and birch. For cheap work give a coat of glue size or painter's size before applying the varnish.

Sycamore.—A close-grained wood, and may be filled or coated with white or orange shellac polish or spirit varnish.

Walnut.—Mix together equal parts of rye flour and china-clay, colouring with burnt umber; mix to a paste with a thinner made from two parts turpentine, one part boiled oil, and two parts japan gold-size. Or mix together 1½ lbs. burnt umber and ¼ lb. burnt sienna, both ground in oil, and add ¼ quart of turpentine and ¼ pint of brown japan driers. Mix to a paste.

One of the best fillers for general work is whiting and plaster-of-paris mixed with turpentine and coloured to the desired tint with the required dry colours. A little gold-size should be added to the mixture to act as a binder.

Appendix

RECIPES FOR VARNISHES.

OIL VARNISHES.

It will be readily understood that to make an oil varnish satisfactorily is not an easy matter without the necessary apparatus, and it is impossible here to adequately explain the different processes adopted in its manufacture. A knowledge of the ingredients of different kinds of varnishes will, however, be of material service to the worker.

Pale Oak Varnish.—11 lbs. of best kauri gum; 9 quarts of clarified linseed oil; 20 ozs. of powdered litharge; 4 ozs. of black oxide of manganese; 15 quarts of American turpentine.

Medium Oak Varnish.—3 gallons of linseed oil; 8 lbs. of copal; 5 gallons of turpentine; 4 ozs. of litharge; 3 ozs. each of sugar of lead and dried copperas.

Copal Varnish.—8 lbs. of pale copal, 3 gallons of raw oil, 2½ gallons of turpentine, and ¾ lb. of litharge.

Resin Varnish.—60 lbs. of pale amber resin, 6 lbs. of thick albumenised oil, ½ lb. of newly slaked lime, and 8 gallons of American turpentine.

Quick-drying Varnish.—A quick-drying oil varnish is made from two parts of oil to one of resin, or one part of oil to two of copal. This is afterwards diluted with hot oil of turpentine to make it sufficiently fluid.

Flatting Varnishes.—4 lbs. of damar gum, 3 quarts of American turpentine, ¾ lb. of beeswax, and ½ oz. of slaked lime.

SPIRIT VARNISHES.

White Hard Varnish.—2 lbs. of sandarac; 1 lb. of gum-thus; 1 gallon of methylated spirit. Some makes of white hard varnish contain mastic.

Brown Hard Varnish.—1 gallon of methylated spirit, 2 lbs. of orange shellac, 8 ozs. of resin, and 4 ozs. of gum benzoin.

Quick-drying Spirit Varnish.—4 ozs. of shellac, 1 oz. of sandarac, 1 oz. of gum-thus, and 1 pint of methylated spirit.

Lustrous Elastic Varnish.—Three parts of resin, six parts of sandarac, twelve parts of shellac, and five parts of turpentine in ninety parts of alcohol.

Appendix

Mastic Varnish.—10 ozs. of gum mastic dissolved in 1 pint of turpentine.

WATER VARNISHES.

Water Varnish may be prepared by boiling together 9 ozs. of shellac, 2 ozs. of borax, and 3 gills of water. Boil until the lac is dissolved. This makes a pale brown varnish. A white varnish may be obtained by using bleached shellac. This varnish dries with a hard gloss, and is fairly waterproof. It may be prepared in any colour by adding aniline dyes soluble in water. It is a good paper varnish.

A Cheap Transparent Varnish may be made from the following: 1 lb. of bleached or white lac, 3½ ozs. of borax, 2 ozs. of Canada balsam, and 3½ pints of water.

Another recipe is as follows: 1 lb. of genuine gum arabic, ¼ lb. of glucose, ¼ lb. of powdered glue size, ¼ lb. of salicylic acid, and 4 pints of water. This varnish dries hard, with an excellent gloss, but is not quite so impervious to water as the first-mentioned recipe.

Water varnishes are of course quite unsuitable for woodwork.

VARIOUS VARNISHES.

Celluloid Varnish.—This is a valuable varnish for protecting metal from the corrosive action of the atmosphere. It forms a good hard film of exceptional transparency. It is an excellent waterproofer of paper. Used in a heavy state, it makes a very fine liquid glue, which will secure almost anything—glass, wood, crockery, leather, etc.

Commercial Celluloid Varnish is made by dissolving, say, two parts of nitro-cellulose (pure cotton treated with nitric and sulphuric acids) in 100 parts of acetone, amyl acetate, or a mixture of alcohol and ether, the addition of 1 or 2 per cent. of castor oil giving flexibility.

Crystal Varnish.—Pure Canada balsam and pale spirits of turpentine in equal parts. Put into a close strong vessel.

Waterproof Varnish for Brass Models.—Shellac, 3 ozs.; alcohol, 1 pint. Dissolve in the ordinary way. Warm the model and apply the varnish quickly.

Varnish for Plaster-of-paris Casts.—¾ oz. of white soap; ¾ oz. of white wax; 2 pints of water. Boil together for a short time. This varnish must be applied cold with a soft brush. It dries readily, and does not sink in.

Appendix

VARNISH FOR TOYS.

3 ozs. sandarac; 1½ ozs. gum copal; 1½ ozs. mastic; ¼ pint turpentine; ½ oz. oil of rosemary; 1 pint methylated spirit. Dissolve on a water bath.

For coloured toys use spirit enamels.

PERFUMED VARNISH.

For imitation Oriental goods dissolve on a water bath—white shellac, 10 ozs.; mastic, 4½ ozs.; elemi, ½ oz.; myrrh, ½ oz.; methylated spirit, 3 pints. When dissolved add ½ oz. of copaiba balsam by stirring it in; then filter through cambric.

POPULAR AND SCIENTIFIC NAMES.

It may, perhaps, be useful here to give the common or popular names of the chemicals employed in the operations of staining and imitating, as few know them by the scientific names used by chemists :—

Acetate of Lead is sugar of lead.

Acetate Acid is wood vinegar or pyroligneous acid, the acid of ordinary vinegar.

Alcohol is pure spirits of wine.

Aqua Regia is nitro-muriatic or nitro-hydrochloric acid.

Biborate of Soda is borax.

Bitartrate of Potash is cream of tartar.

Carbonate, Subcarbonate, or Sesquioxide of Iron is pure iron rust.

Chloride or Hydrochloride of Ammonium is sal ammoniac.

Chlorine is a gas obtained by the action of hydrochloric acid on chlorate of potash; water forms " solution of chlorine."

Ferrocyanide or ferroprussiate of Iron is Prussian blue.

Nitrate of Potash is saltpetre, nitre, or sal prunella.

Nitrate of Silver is lunar caustic.

Nitric Acid is aquafortis.

Oxychloride of Bismuth is flake white or pearl white.

Pearl Ash is impure carbonate of potash or commercial salts of tartar.

Appendix

Plumbago is blacklead or graphite.

Sesquicarbonate of Ammonia is lump ammonia, volatile salt, or sal volatile.

Spirit of Hartshorn is solution of ammonia.

Subacetate of Copper is common verdigris.

Sulphate of Copper is blue stone, blue vitriol, or Roman vitriol.

Sulphate of Iron is copperas or green copperas.

Sulphate of Lime is plaster-of-paris or gypsum.

Sulphate of Magnesia is Epsom salts.

Sulphate of Zinc is white copperas or white vitriol.

Sulphuric Acid is vitriol or oil of vitriol.

Superoxalate of Potash is salts of sorrel or salts of lemon.

Yellow Arsenic (pulverised) is king's yellow or yellow sulphide of arsenic.

INDEX

A — cutting stencil letter, 143, 144, 145
Acetate, amyl, 196
Acetate of lead, 128
Acetic acid, 7
Acetone, 196
Acid, acetic, 7
Acid, hydrochloric, 130
Acid, nitric, 7, 25, 127, 185, 187, 188, 196
Acid or refined finish in polishing, 72
Acid, oxalic, 25, 108, 109, 126, 132
Acid, picric, 7
Acid, sulphuric, 72, 186, 196
Adam frame, carved, 86
African gum copal, 154
Albumenised oil, 195
Alcohol, 155, 191, 195, 196
Alderwood, 25
Alkaline dyes, 6
Alkaline manganates, 7
Alkanet root, 88, 192
Almond oil, 88, 192
Alum, 27, 131, 186, 188
Aluminium, 29
Amber, 155
Amboyna wood, 9, 56
American oak, 54, 129, 131
American potash, 95, 96, 184
American whitewood, 9, 10, 31, 56, 183
American whitewood for staining, 31, 183
American whitewood, stains for (recipes), 183
Ammonia, 25, 95, 125, 128, 130, 183, 184
Amyl acetate, 196
Anaglypta, 23
Aniline dyes, 6, 7, 20, 188
Aniline green, 129
Aniline powders, 7
Animi, gum-, 111
Antimony, butter of, 102, 179, 193

Antique furniture, dull finish on, 80
Antique oak, 128
Appendix of recipes, 183—198
Apple wood, 9, 27
Arabic, gum, 196
Archil dye, 188
Arsenate of copper, 7
Arsenic, yellow, 187
Ash, 9, 54, 56, 61, 193
Ash, black, 95
Ash filler, 193
Asphaltum, 7, 130, 184, 194
Atmosphere, seaside—effect on polished work, 110
Atmospheric moisture, 102

BAG, muslin, 88
Bag, pounce, 44, 48, 58, 69, 128
Ballroom floors, polishing, 136
Balsam, 196, 197
Baltic linseed oil, 153
Barytes, 162
Basswood, 10
Bath brick, 107, 127
Baywood, 34, 88, 183
Baywood, staining, 34, 183
Baywood, treatment of, 34
Beadings, removing before polishing, 49
Beaumontage (hard stopping), 14, 52
Beech, 9, 29, 193
Beech filler, 193
Beer, 183, 186
Beeswax, 7, 38, 43, 52, 83, 109, 122, 137, 195
Beeswax and turpentine for wax-polishing, 137
Bengal blue, 29
Benzine, 11
Benzoin, 72, 77, 81, 82, 84, 111, 122, 190, 191, 195
Benzolene, 56, 96, 106, 108, 110, 111, 153, 170, 178

Index

Bichromate of potash, 35, 90, 127, 128, 183, 184, 185
Birch, 9, 25, 32, 54, 56, 183, 193
Birch, American, 9
Birch filler, 193
Birch, staining, 32
Birch, treatment of, 32, 183
Bird's eye maple, 118
Bismarck brown, 19, 29, 32, 33, 69, 115, 183, 186, 189, 194
Black ash, 95
Black, Berlin, 96
Black, Brunswick, 149, 184
Black, drop, 33, 128, 129, 185, 194
Black, gas, 27, 56, 96, 190
Black, ivory, 186
Black japan, 7, 151, 180
Black, lamp, 7, 56, 69, 89, 186, 187, 193
Black oak, 91
Black polish, 185, 191
Black, spirit, 129
Black stain, French, 27, 28
Black, vegetable, 69, 89, 127
Bleached oak, 131
Bleached shellac, 40, 61, 84, 190, 193, 194, 196
Bleaching dark patches in staining, 25
Blended stains, 150
Blistering on varnished work, 176
Blisters on polished work, 106
Blisters on veneered work, removing, 99
Blood, dragon's, 7, 155, 187
Bloom on varnished work, 166, 175
Blue, Bengal, 29
Blue black, 6
Blue copperas, 34, 187
Blue de lumière, 29
Blue dye, 89
Blue, Prussian, 186, 187, 190
Blue, Reckitt's, 129
Blue, spirit, 129
Blue stain, 29
Blue stains (self-colours), recipes for, 186
Bodying-in, 62

Bodying-up, 65
Boiled linseed oil, 56, 122, 133, 185, 193, 194
Boiling water, varnish to resist, 155
Bone charcoal, 73
Bookcase, 60
Borax, 156, 196
Bottle—holding with one hand, 76
Bottles for polishing, etc., 43
Box, polishing inlaid, 113
Boxes—holding for polishing, 74
Boxwood, 9
Brackets—holding for polishing, 75
Brasswork—removing ⋆ before polishing, 49, 96
Brazilwood, 7, 185, 187, 188
Brick, bath, 107, 127
Brooke's soap, 127
Brown, bismarck, 19, 29, 32, 33, 69, 115, 183, 186, 189
Brown japan, 128, 193, 194
Brown madder, 128, 187
Brown polish, 85, 190
Brown stain, 29
Brown stains (self-colours), recipes for, 187
Brown umber, 56
Brown, vandyke, 6, 19, 33, 69, 89, 90, 91, 96, 97, 116, 118, 127, 128, 162, 184, 187, 194
Bruises on polished oak, 105
Brunswick black, 149, 184
Brunswick green, 34
Brush, camel hair, 43, 89
Brush for filling, 59
Brush, gilder's mop, 43, 59, 89
Brush, nail, 83
Brush polish (recipe), 190
Brush, stencil, 143
Brushes, 17—20, 43, 59, 70, 83, 89, 143, 163, 164, 165, 172
Brushes for spirit varnishing, 172
Brushes for staining, 17, 18, 19, 20
Brushes to be kept in a tin, 59
Brushes, varnish, 163, 164, 165, 172
Brushwork in staining, 15

200

Index

Burns on veneered work, removing, 100
Burnt sienna, 6, 32, 183, 185, 186, 187, 193, 194
Burnt umber, 6, 32, 37, 89, 90, 91, 128, 186, 194
Butter of antimony, 102, 179, 193
Button lac, 122, 189
Button polish, 32, 33, 189

CABINET, china, 60
Cabinet, oak, 182
Cabinet, stationery, with marquetry transfer, 132
Cabinets, etc., dry-shining for inside parts of, 80
Calico, 43
Californian redwood, 9
Cambric, 127, 181
Camel hair brush, 43, 89
Campeachy wood, 27
Camphor, 155, 193
Canary (*see* American whitewood), 9, 10, 56, 183
Canister, airtight, for rubbers, 64
Canisters for materials, 43
Canoe wood, 31
Carriages, varnish for, 153, 157
Cartridge paper for stencils, 144
Carved Adam frame, 86
Carved picture frame (Gothic), 141
Carved pipe rack, 142
Carved work, cleaning out, 95
Carved work, dull polishing, 82
Carved work, repairing damaged, 100
Carved work, sizing, 12
Carved work, staining, 24
Carving, substitutes for, 23
Carvings, antique stain on oak, 24
Carvings, dull polishing fumed oak, 83
Carvings, overlay, removing before polishing, 49
Carvings, polishing applied, 75
Castor oil, 196
Cathedral oak (stained), 128

Caustic soda, 30
Cedar, 9
Celluloid varnish, recipe for, 196
Chairs, preparing for polishing, 51
Chalk, French, 137
Chalk, Vienna, 72
Chamois leather, 178, 179
Charcoal, bone, 73
Chart, colour, for staining, 20
Cheap stains, 5, 6
Cheese cloth, 129, 163
Chemical staining, 4
Chemical stains, 7
Chemical stains (*see also* Recipes).
Cherry wood, 9, 27, 29, 193
Cherry wood filler, 193
Cherry wood stains, recipes, 186
Chestnut, 9, 116, 193
Chestnut filler, 193
China cabinet, 60
China clay, 56, 194
Chipped woodwork, repairing, 100
Chippendale mahogany stains, recipes for, 184
Chippendale work, old, 92
Chocolate stains (self-colours), recipes for, 187
Chroma, 35, 90
Chrome, 84, 89, 129, 186, 187, 188
Church oak varnish, 157
Church seats, varnishing, 159
Cissing on varnished work, 170, 176
Clay, china, 56, 194
Cleaning old woodwork, 97, 98
Clocks, old grandfather, 93
Coal-tar naphtha, 130
Coal-tar spirit, 153, 154, 155
Coating, double, in varnishing, 181
Coating, water, 4, 7
Coating, water, recipes for, 186
Coburg varnish, 32, 157
Cochineal, 7, 187
Coffin plinths, elm, 131
Coffins—holding for polishing, 74
Coffins, polishing oak, 130

201

Index

Colour chart for staining, 20
Colour schemes in staining, 22, 23
Coloured effects in staining, 147—150
Coloured fillers for staining, 13
Coloured stains for wicker work, 29
Colouring in polishing, 69
Colouring, sap, 89
Colouring-up in matching, 90
Colourless varnish, 84
Colours for polishing fillers, 56
Colours for spirit enamelling, 84
Colours, self-, recipes for, 186, 187, 188
Copal, African gum, 154
Copal, gum, 102, 152, 153, 154, 155, 191, 195, 197
Copal varnish, 32, 110, 157, 174, 180, 195
Copal varnish, recipe for, 195
Copper, 29
Copper, arsenate of, 7
Copper, subacetate of, 7
Copperas, 34, 185, 187, 195
Coral red, 29
Cornflour, 56, 141
Cotton rag, 43
Cotton-seed oil, 153
Cotton wadding, 43
Cottonwood, 10
Cracking on varnished work, 176
Cracks on polished work, 102, 103, 104
Creeping on varnished work, 177
Crimson lake, 187, 188
Crimson stains (self-colours), recipes for, 187
Cuban mahogany, 34, 35
Curdling on varnished work, 178

DAMAR, gum, 153, 195
Darkeners for staining, 25
Darkening oak, 91, 127, 128
Deal, white, 9
Deal, yellow, 9
Defects in polishing and their remedies, 101—111
Dents in veneered work, removing, 100

Design in staining, 147—150
Diamond dyes, 20
Direct filling with polish, 57
Disabled men—methods of supporting work for, 73—76
Dolly dyes, 20
Double coating in varnishing, 181
Dragon's blood, 7, 155, 187
Drawers, holding for polishing, 74
Dressing wood, 12, 13
Dried copperas, 195
Drier, japan, 129
Drier, patent, 56
Drop black, 33, 128, 129, 185, 194
Dry shining, 79, 80
Drying, varnish not, 178
Dull varnished surfaces, 178
Dulling polished work, 80
Dulness on polished work, 106
Dust, to guard against, in varnishing, 167
Dusters, hot, 102
Dusting prior to varnishing, 168
Dyed (impregnated) wood, 25
Dyed oil, 25
Dyeing woods and veneers, 29
Dyes, alkaline, 6
Dyes, aniline, 6, 7, 20, 188
Dyes, diamond, 20
Dyes, dolly, 20
Dyes for ebony staining, 27

EARTH, fuller's, 162
Ebonised work, dull finish on, 80
Ebonising, 26, 27
Ebonising, woods for, 27
Ebony, 9, 56, 193
Ebony filler, 193
Ebony stains, 26, 27
Ebony stains, recipes for, 185
Ebony, woods to use for imitating, 10
Egg-shell gloss, 80
Elastic varnishes, 158, 159
Elemi, 197
Elm, 54, 56, 194
Elm coffin plinths, 131
Elm filler, 194
Emery, 81, 96

Index

Enamelling, 83
Enamelling, spirit, colours for, 84
Enamels, 151
Enamels, spirit, 172, 197
Epsom salts, 184
Equipment, polishing, 43
Ether, 196

FADDING-IN, 62
Fading on polished work, 107
Fatting, 62
Faults in varnishing and their remedies, 175—179
Faulty polish, causing cracks, 104
Felt, 43
Felt for dull-polishing, 81
Felt rubber, 170
Felting down, 169, 170
Filings, iron, 128, 185
Filler for intarsia work, 117, 118
Filler for spirit enamelling, 84
Filler for veneered and inlaid work, 115
Fillers, brush for, 59
Fillers, coloured, for staining, 13
Fillers for cheap work, 59
Fillers for polishing, 54—57
Fillers for polishing, applying, 57
Fillers for staining, 13
Fillers, polishing, colours for, 56
Fillers, recipes for, 193, 194
Fillers, varnish or polish, 59
Filling for fretwork polishing, 123
Filling-in for turned work, 122
Filling with polish direct, 57
Finger-marks on polished work, 106
Finger-marks on varnished work, 178
Fir, red, Scotch and white, 9
Fitch, hog hair, 18
Flake white, 84
Flaking on varnished work, 177
Flatting varnish, 174
Flatting varnish, recipe for, 195
Flemish oak (stained), 128
Floor margins, staining, 37, 38
Floor margins, varnishing, 173

Floor polish, 192
Floors, oil-polishing, 136
Floors, polishing ballroom, 136
Floors, stains for, 37, 38
Floors, wax-polishing, 142
Flour, rye, 194
Frame, carved Gothic, 141
Frame, mirror or picture, carved, 86
Frames, picture, spirit enamelling for, 86
French black stain, 27, 28
French chalk, 137
French oil varnish, 157
French polish, recipes for, 189, 190
French polishing, 39—76
    acid or refined method of, 72
    acquiring skill in, 40, 41
    bodying-in, 62
    bodying-up, 65
    colouring, 69
    defects in, 101—110
    equipment, the, 43
    fatting, 62
    fillers, applying, 57
    fillers, colours for, 56
    fillers for, 54—57
    filling direct with polish, 57
    glass-papering before, 51
    glazing, 72, 77
    oiling, preliminary, 62
    old methods, 41
    preparing furniture for, 49
    processes, 61—76
    refined or acid, method of, 72
    room, the, 42
    rubbers, 44—48
    rubbers, charging, 46
    rubbers, holding, 47, 66
    rubbers, making, 44
    rubbers, movements of, 66, 67
    rubbers, spirit, 71
    rubbers, wrapping, 45
    scraping before, 51
    shellac, 39, 40
    sizing in, 62
    skill in, acquiring, 40, 41

Index

French polishing—*contd.*
  spiriting-out, 70
  stiffing-up, 71, 72
  stopping, 52
  supporting work for, 73—76
  wax stopping, 52, 53
  what it is, 40
  wood, preparing, 49
  working-up, 65
  workshop, the, 42
French polishing (*see also* under Polishing).
Fretted articles, spirit varnish for, 172
Fretwork, overglazing on, 24
Fretwork, polishing, 123
Fuller's earth, 162
Fumed oak, 148
Fumed oak stain, 129
Fumigating box or chamber, 125
Fuming, or fumigating, 125
Funnel, wide-nosed, 181
Furniture, chipped or with holes, repaired with wax, 100
Furniture, dry-shining for inside parts of, 80
Furniture (ebonised and antique), dull finish on, 80
Furniture, preparing for French polishing, 49
Furniture repairs, 98
Furniture, repolishing, 92, 96
Furniture revivers, recipes for, 193
Furniture, treating interior parts of, 82
Furniture, upholstered, preparing for polishing, 50
Furniture, washing, 98
Fustic, 187

GALL nuts, 185, 187
Gall, ox, 73, 107
Gamboge, 6, 185
Garnet polish (recipe), 189
Garnet shellac, 189
Gas black, 27, 56, 96, 190
Gelatine, 120
Gilder's mop, 43, 59, 89
Glass, broken, 154

Glass, removing before polishing 49
Glass-paper, 43, 62, 93, 94, 96, 106, 107, 173
Glass-papering, 11, 51, 58
Glass, plate, 179
Glaze, 72, 77
Glaze, preparation of, 72, 190
Glazing 72, 77
Glazing—overglazing, 24
Glazing, rubber for, 79
Gloss, egg-shell, 80
Glucose, 196
Glue size, 12, 84, 148, 161, 173, 196
Glue size for dressing wood, 12
Glycerine, 105
Gold size, japanner's, 12, 32, 185, 193, 194
Golden oak, dark, 184
Golden varnish, 155
Golden yellow stain, 29
Gothic frame, carved, 141
Grain filling (*see* Fillers and Filling).
Grain imitation in matching, 91
Grain in veneers, 118
Grand piano music rests, polishing, 124
Grandfather clocks, old, 93
Grease marks, 11
Green, aniline, 129
Green, Brunswick, 34
Green, chrome, 129
Green copperas, 185
Green dye, 89
Green, methyl, 29
Green oak, stained, 129
Green stain, 29
Green stains (self-colours), recipes for, 187
Greenheart, 9
Grey, silver, oak (stained), 130
Grey stains (self-colours), recipes for, 187
Grittiness on varnished work, 177
Gum animi, 111
Gum arabic, 196
Gum, benzoin, 72, 77, 111, 122

Index

Gum, copal, 102, 152, 153, 154, 155, 191, 195, 197
Gum copal, African, 154
Gum damar, 153, 195
Gum juniper, 189
Gum mastic, 61, 84, 191, 195, 196, 197
Gum sandarac, 84, 122
Gums (recipes), 191
Gum-thus, 195

HANDLES, removing, before polishing, 49
Hard polish, causing cracks, 103
Hard stopping, 14, 52
Hard varnish, white, 150
Hard varnishes, 157, 158, 159
Hard woods, 9
Hazelwood, 10
Hinges, removing, before polishing, 49
Holes in woodwork, filling, 100
Holes, stopping, before polishing, 52
Holly, 9, 27, 29, 61
Honduras mahogany, 35, 88
Hooks, shave, 95
Hornbeam, 25
Hydrochloric acid, 130

IMPREGNATED wood, 25
Improving (*see* Matching).
Indian red, 187
Indiana oak, 131
Indiarubber solutions, 158
Indigo, 6, 7, 186, 187
Ink, shoemaker's, 184, 185
Ink stains on polished work, 109
Inlaid box, polishing, 113
Inlaid panel, Japanese, 112
Inlaid Sheraton table, polishing, 115
Inlaid work, polishing, 113
Inlaid work, use of chroma for, 35
Inlay transfer, stationery cabinet with, 132
Inlay work, example of, 111
Inlay work (*see also* Marquetry and Veneers).

Inlays, polishing pictorial (intarsia), 116
Intarsia, polishing, 116
Iron, 29
Iron filings, 128, 185
Iron, hot, to remove scratches, 107
Iron, sulphate of, 7, 25, 185
Isinglass size, 162
Italian walnut, 9, 36
Italian walnut, treatment of, 36
Ivory black, 186

JAPAN black, 7, 151, 180
Japan, brown, 128, 193, 194
Japan drier, 129
Japan gold size, 12, 32, 185, 193, 194
Japan (mahogany), 194
Japanese, inlaid panel, 112
Japanner's varnish, 156
Jar for varnish brushes, 164
Jars for materials, 43
Jasper, 9
Johnson's fumed oak stain, 129
Johnson's stains, 6, 129
Johnson's wax, 192
Juniper, 84, 189

KAURI gum, 195
Kerosine, 184
Knives, stencil, 145, 146
Knobs, polishing, 121
Knotting, 18, 146, 148, 149

LAC, button, 122, 189
Lac, seed, 39
Lac, stick, 39
Lacewood, 9
Lacquers, 96, 158
Lake, crimson, 187, 188
Lake, mahogany, 6, 38, 186, 187
Lake, red, 33, 186
Lake, yellow, 6
Lamp black, 7, 56, 69, 89, 186, 187, 193
Lead, acetate of, 128
Lead, red, 155, 162
Lead, sugar of, 195
Leather, chamois, 178, 179
Lemon chrome, 89
Light for hardening varnish, 180

Index

Lignomur, 23
Lime as a darkener, 25, 195
Lime water, 102
Lime wood, 9
Lincrusta-walton, 23
Linseed oil, Baltic, 153
Linseed oil, boiled, 56, 122, 133, 185, 193, 194
Linseed oil, choice of, for varnishes, 154
Linseed oil, clarified, 195
Linseed oil, raw, 32, 33, 58, 62, 85, 88, 97, 102, 103, 105, 106, 107, 108, 109, 116, 130, 133, 152, 153, 162, 170, 179, 180, 183, 184, 192, 193, 194
Linseed oils, varying qualities of, 152
Litharge, 155, 194, 195
Logwood, 7, 25, 27, 184, 185, 187
Lustre, lack of, on varnished work, 177

MADDER, brown, 128, 187
Magnolia, 31
Mahogany, 10, 24, 29, 31, 54, 56, 62, 88, 89, 115, 137, 183, 194
Mahogany, American whitewood for imitating, 31
Mahogany, bay (or baywood), 34, 88, 183
Mahogany, Chippendale, recipe for, 184
Mahogany, Cuban, 34, 35
Mahogany, Cuban and Spanish, treatment of, 35
Mahogany filler, 194
Mahogany, Honduras, 35, 88
Mahogany lake, 6, 38, 186, 187
Mahogany, Sheraton, recipe for, 183
Mahogany, Spanish, 9, 35, 88
Mahogany stains, recipes for, 183, 184
Mander's stains, 6
Manganates, alkaline, 7
Manganese, black oxide of, 195
Maple, 9, 54, 56, 116
Maple, bird's-eye, 118, 194
Maple filler, 194

Maple stains, recipes for, 185
Maple varnish, 157
Maps, varnish for, 157
Marble varnish, white, 157
Marks, finger, on polished work, 106
Marks, finger, on varnished work, 178
Marks, grease, 11
Marks, hot plate or jug, on polished work, 110
Marks, pock, etc., on varnished work, 176
Marks, salt, on polished work, 110
Marks, water, on polished work, 109
Marks, white, on polished work, 108
Marquetry (*see also* Inlay, Inlaying and Veneers).
Marquetry and inlaid work, polishing, 113
Marquetry (intarsia), polishing, 116
Marquetry transfer, stationery cabinet with, 132
Marquetry transfers, 119
Mastic gum, 61, 84, 191, 195, 196, 197
Mastic varnish, 157, 196
Matching and improving, 87
    colouring-up, 90
    grain imitation, 91
    oiling, 88
    sap colouring, 89
    stained polish, 89
Matching in staining, 25
Methyl green, 29
Methyl violet, 29
Methylated finish, causing cracks, 104
Methylated spirit, 48, 55, 59, 61, 77, 82, 84, 85, 93, 102, 104, 105, 110, 111, 115, 118, 120, 122, 127, 129, 131, 150, 153, 156, 179, 183, 185, 186, 187, 188, 189, 190, 191, 193, 195, 197
Methylated spirit (*see also* Appendix, page 191).
Minium (red lead), 155

Index

Mirror frame, carved, 86
Mirrors—removing before polishing, 49
Mission oak (stained), 129
Moisture, atmospheric, 102
Moisture, excessive, a cause of whiteness, 108
Monkey soap, 102
Mop, gilder's, 43, 59, 89
Mordants, 29
Mottled woods, imitating, 91
Mouldings, cleaning out, 95
Mouldings, dull-polishing, 82
Mouldings — removing before polishing, 49
Music rests, grand pianos, polishing, 124
Muslin, 84, 181, 192
Muslin bag, 88
Muslin for staining, 43
Myrrh, 197

NAIL brush, 83
Naphtha, 104, 184, 188
Naphtha, coal-tar, 130
Naphtha, mineral, 153
Naphtha, varnish, 131, 157
Naphtha, wood, 131, 153
Naphthaline, yellow, 29
New wood, varnishing, 161
Nitrate of silver, 25, 130
Nitric acid, 7, 25, 127, 185, 187, 188, 196
Nitro-cellulose, 196
Nut oils, 153

OAK, 9, 10, 24, 54, 56, 61, 64, 83, 89, 91, 96, 97, 116, 117, 118, 125—132, 137, 148, 184, 194
Oak, American, 54, 129, 131
Oak and its various finishes—
    antique oak, 128
    bleached oak, 131
    cathedral oak, 128
    dark oak, 127
    Flemish oak, 128
    fuming, 125
    green oak, 129
    grey (silver) oak, 130
    mission oak, 129
    oak coffins, 130

Oak, antique, 128
Oak, black, 91
Oak cabinet, 182
Oak carvings, antique shade on, 24
Oak carvings, dull-polishing fumed, 83
Oak, cathedral (stained), 128
Oak coffins, polishing, 130
Oak, dark golden, 184
Oak, darkening, 91, 127, 128
Oak, ebonising, 27
Oak filler, recipe for, 194
Oak, Flemish (stained), 128
Oak, fumed, 148
Oak, fumigating, 125
Oak, green (stained), 129
Oak—handling in polishing, 64
Oak, how to bleach, 131
Oak, Indiana, 131
Oak, mission (stained), 129
Oak, restoring old, 96, 97
Oak, silver grey (stained), 130
Oak stain, 33
Oak stain, fumed, 129
Oak stains, recipes for, 184
Oak varnishes, 157
Oak varnishes, recipes for, 195
Ochre, 7, 32, 33, 56, 89, 90, 118, 131, 132, 186, 187, 188, 194
Oil, 101
Oil, albumenised, 195
Oil, almond, 88, 192
Oil, Baltic linseed, 153
Oil, boiled linseed, 56, 122, 133, 185, 193, 194
Oil, castor, 196
Oil, cotton-seed, 153
Oil, dyed, 25
Oil, excessive, causing grease marks, 106
Oil, linseed, choice of, for varnishes, 154
Oil, olive, 175
Oil, paraffin, 56, 102, 184
Oil, petroleum, 102
Oil polishing, 133
Oil, poppy, 106, 111, 192
Oil, preliminary use of, for polishing, 62

Index

Oil, preparing, for oil-polishing, 134
Oil, raw linseed, 32, 33, 58, 62, 85, 88, 97, 102, 103, 105, 106, 107, 108, 109, 116, 130, 133, 152, 153, 162, 170, 179, 180, 183, 184, 192, 194
Oil, red, 25, 62, 88, 89, 183
Oil staining, 4
Oil stains, 4, 7
Oil stains (see Recipes).
Oil, sweet, 88, 178
Oil varnish for dressing wood, 13
Oil-varnished work, 104
Oil varnishes, 157, 158
Oiling as a means of darkening and improving, 88
Oils, cotton, rape and fish, for varnishes, 153
Oils, linseed, varying qualities of, 152
Oils, nut, 153
Oils (see also Appendix, page 192).
Old oak, restoring, 96, 97
Olive oil, 175
Olive wood, 9
One-handed polishers, 76
Orange chrome, 89
Orange shellac, 52, 61, 85, 128, 183, 189, 190, 194, 195
Orange stains (self-colours), recipes for, 187
Orange wood, 9
Ordinary polish, 61, 190
Ornamental wood staining, 143, 147—150
   leaving plain panel on stained ground, 147
   obtaining different depths of stain, 150
   pattern with dark outline, 149
   pattern with light outline, 149
   polychromatic effect, 149
   putting solid colour on stained ground or plain wood, 148
   stencil of blended stains, 150
Outdoor polished and varnished work, 174

Overglazing, 24
Oxalic acid, 25, 108, 109, 126, 132
Ox-gall, 73, 107
Oxide of manganese, black, 195

PAD, spiriting, 71
Padouk, 116, 117, 118
Painted work, varnishing, 162
Paintings, mastic varnish for, 157
Panel, inlaid Japanese, 112
Panelled stained work, 147—150
Panels, staining, 15, 16
Panels, supporting, 74
Paper, cartridge, for stencils, 144
Paper varnish, 156, 157
Paraffin, 56, 102, 184
Paraffin causing patches, 109
Paraffin wax, 148
Parchment size, 84
Patches, faulty, on varnished work, 175
Patchiness on polished work, 109
Patent drier, 56
Patent stains, 7, 8
Pattern staining, 147—150
Pear wood, 9, 24, 27
Pearlash, 34, 184, 187, 188
Peeling on varnished work, 177
Pencils (brushes), 43, 149
Perfumed varnish, recipe for, 197
Perishing on varnished work, 177
Permanganate of potash, 7, 38, 128, 184, 185
Petroleum, 153
Petroleum oil, 102
Piano (grand) music rests, polishing, 124
Pianos, method of finishing, 73
Pianos, preparing for polishing, 50
Picric acid, 7
Pictorial inlays, polishing, 116
Picture frame, carved Gothic, 141
Picture frames, spirit enamelling for, 86
Picture or mirror frame, carved, 86

Index

Pictures, mastic varnish for, 157
Pillars, polishing small, 121
Pine, 9, 24, 31, 32, 183, 194
Pine, Canadian, 9
Pine, canary, 31
Pine filler, recipe for, 194
Pine, kauri, 9, 31
Pine, northern, 9
Pine, pitch, 9, 24, 32
Pine, pitch, staining, 32
Pine, to darken, 32
Pine, treatment of, 31, 32
Pine, yellow, 9
Pinholing on varnished work, 176
Pink, rose, 7, 56, 129, 186
Pipe rack, carved, 142
Pitch pine, 9, 24, 32
Pitch pine, staining, 32
Pitting on varnished work, 176
Plane wood, 9
Plaster-of-paris, 32, 43, 55, 56, 57, 108, 193, 194
Plaster-of-paris, finely ground, 57
Plate glass, 179
Plate, stencil, 144
Plum wood, 24
Pock marks on varnished work, 176
Poker, hot iron, 105
Polish and varnish fillers, 59
Polish, black, 185, 191
Polish, brown, 85
Polish, button, 32, 33
Polish, direct filling with, 57
Polish, faulty—causing cracks, 104
Polish, floor, 192
Polish, hard—causing cracks, 103
Polish, ordinary, 61
Polish, red, 83, 184, 191
Polish, removing old, 93
Polish, stained, for matching, 89
Polish, waterproof, 111
Polish, wax, 138
Polish, white, 32, 61, 115
Polish, yellow, 96, 97
Polished work, dulling, 80
Polishers, single-handed, 76

Polishes, recipes for, 188—192
Polishing (*see also* French Polishing, Oil Polishing, Re-polishing, and Wax Polishing).
Polishing applied carvings, 75
Polishing, applying fillers, 57
Polishing, bodying-in, 62
Polishing, bodying-up, 65
Polishing, colouring, 69
Polishing, colours for fillers, 56
Polishing defects and their remedies—
 blisters, 106
 bruises, 105
 cracks, 102, 103, 104
 dulness, 106
 fading, 107
 finger marks, 106
 patchiness, 109
 salt marks, 110
 scratches, 107
 stains, 109
 sweating, 101
 water marks, 110
 whiteness, 108
Polishing equipment, the, 43
Polishing, fatting or bodying in, 62
Polishing, French, 39—76
Polishing fretwork, 123
Polishing, holding bottle with one hand, 76
Polishing, incorrect movements of rubber, 68
Polishing inlaid work, 113
Polishing, movements of rubber, 66, 67
Polishing oak coffins, 130
Polishing, oil, 133—137
Polishing, refined or acid finish, 72
Polishing rubber, the, 44—48
Polishing, spiriting, 70
Polishing, supporting work for, 73—76
Polishing turned work, 121
Polishing, wax, 137—142
Polishing, wax-, floors, 142
Polishing, working up, 65
Polishing workshop, the, 42

Index

Polychromatic effects in staining, 149
Poplar, 9, 31
Poppy oil, 106, 111, 192
Popular and scientific names of media, 197, 198
Pores (*see* Fillers and Filling).
Potash, 29
Potash, American, 95, 96, 184
Potash, bichromate of, 35, 90, 127, 128, 183, 184, 185
Potash, permanganate of, 7, 38, 184, 185
Pots for polishes, etc., 43
Pounce bag, 44, 48, 58, 69, 128
Powdered wax, 137
Powders, aniline, 7
Preparing wood, 10
Prints, varnish for, 157
Prussian blue, 186, 187, 190
Pumice, 56, 58, 69, 81, 85, 97, 102, 104, 107, 110, 111, 116, 129, 130, 136, 170, 194
Pumice stone, 43, 96
Purple stains (self-colours), recipes for, 187
Puttying for staining, 14

QUICK-DRYING varnish, recipes for, 195

RAG, cotton, 43
Raw linseed oil, 32, 33, 58, 62, 85, 88, 97, 102, 103, 105, 106, 107, 108, 109, 116, 130, 133, 152, 153, 162, 170, 179, 180, 183, 184, 192, 193, 194, 195
Raw sienna, 6, 38, 118, 184, 185, 187
Raw umber, 6, 32, 128
Recipes for fillers, stains, polishes, varnishes, etc., 183—198
Recipes for fillers—
 ash, 193
 beech, 193
 birch, 193
 cherry, 193
 chestnut, 193
 ebony, 193

Recipes for fillers—*contd.*
 elm, 194
 mahogany, 194
 maple, 194
 oak, 194
 pine, 194
 satin walnut, 194
 sycamore, 194
 walnut, 194
Recipes for furniture revivers, 193
Recipes for polishes :—
 brown polish, 190
 brush polish, 190
 button polish, 189
 dark polish, 189
 French polish, 189, 190
 garnet polish, 189
 glaze, 190
 gums, 191
 orange polish, 190
 transparent polish, 190
 white polish, 190
Recipes for stains :—
 cherry wood, 186
 coating, water, 186
 colours, self-, 186, 187, 188
 ebony, 185
 mahogany, 183, 184
 mahogany (Chippendale), 184
 mahogany (for American whitewood), 183
 mahogany (Sheraton), 183
 maple, 185
 oak, 184
 rosewood, 184, 185
 satinwood, 185
 self-colours, 186, 187, 188
 walnut, 184
 water coating, 186
Recipes for varnishes (oil), 195
Recipes for varnishes (spirit), 195, 196
Recipes for varnishes (various), 196, 197
Recipes for varnishes (water), 196
Reckitt's blue, 129
Red, coral, 29
Red, Indian, 187
Red lake, 33, 186

Index

Red lead, 155, 162
Red oil, 25, 62, 88, 89, 183
Red polish, 83, 184, 191
Red stain, 29
Red stains (self-colours), recipes for, 188
Red, Venetian, 7, 38, 56, 89, 116, 118, 131, 183, 184, 186, 193
Redwood, Brazilian, 7
Redwood, Californian, 9
Refined or acid finish in polishing, 72
Relief material, staining, 23
Removing old polish, 93
Removing old varnish, 94, 95
Renovating wax-polished surfaces, 142
Repairs, furniture, 98
Repolishing furniture, 92, 96
Resin, 52, 84, 137, 139, 191, 195
Resin and wax, 139
Resin, powdered, 52
Resin varnish, recipe for, 195
Resin, yellow, 84
Restoring furniture, 92
Revarnishing, 163
Reviver for sweating, 102
Revivers, furniture, recipes for, 193
Rock ammonia, 95
Roman vitriol, 7
Ronuk, 142, 192
Room, the polishing, 42
Root, alkanet, 88, 192
Ropey surface on varnished work, 178
Rosemary, 197
Rose pink, 7, 56, 129, 186
Rosewood, 9, 31, 35, 36, 54, 56, 184
Rosewood, American whitewood for imitating, 31
Rosewood stain, 33
Rosewood stains, recipes for, 184, 185
Rosewood, treatment of, 36
Rottenstone, 43
Rubber for fretwork polishing, 123, 124
Rubber for glazing, 79

Rubber for turned work, 122
Rubber for wax-polishing, 140
Rubber, how to hold the, 47, 66
Rubber, incorrect movements of, 68
Rubber—keeping in airtight tin, 64
Rubber, movements of, 66, 67
Rubber, spirit, 71
Rubber, the polishing, 44—48
Russian tallow, 33, 56
Rye flour, 194

SADDLETREE, 31
Saffron, 7, 155
Salicylic acid, 196
Salt, 7
Salt marks on polished work, 110
Salts, Epsom, 184
Sandarac, 61, 78, 84, 111, 122, 156, 191, 195, 197
Sanders' wood, 7, 183, 186, 188, 189
Sandpapering (*see* Glass-papering).
Sap colouring, 89
Satin walnut, 9, 33, 61, 64, 116, 194
Satin walnut, filler for, 194
Satin walnut, treatment of, 33
Satinwood, 9, 54, 56, 115
Satinwood stains, recipes for, 185
Scarlet stains (self-colours), recipes for, 188
Scientific and popular names of media, 197, 198
Scraper, 51, 94, 115
Scraper, decorator's, 94
Scratches on polished work, 107
Scratches on veneered work, 100
Scumbling, 23
Seaside atmosphere, effect on polished work, 110
Seats, varnishing church, 159
Seed lac, 39
Self-colours, recipes for, 186, 187, 188
Sequoia, 9
Shapings—holding for polishing, 75

211

Index

Shave hooks, 95
Shavings, wood, for turned work, 121
Shellac, 39, 43, 104, 156, 189, 195, 196, 197
Shellac, adulterated, 102
Shellac bleached, 40, 61, 84, 190, 193, 194, 196
Shellac, garnet, 189
Shellac, orange, 52, 61, 85, 128, 183, 189, 190, 194, 195
Shellac varnish (knotting), 146
Shellac, what it is, 39
Shellac, white, 40, 130, 194, 197
Sheraton mahogany stains, recipes for, 183
Sheraton table, polishing inlaid, 115
Sheraton transfers, 120
Shields, spirit enamelling for decorative, 85
Shining, dry, 79, 80
Shoemaker's ink, 184, 185
Sienna (*see* Burnt Sienna and Raw Sienna).
Sieve, 84
Silica, 193, 194
Silver grey oak (stained), 130
Silver, nitrate, 25, 130
Single-handed polishers, 76
Size, glue, 84, 148, 161, 173, 196
Size, glue, for dressing wood, 12
Size, isinglass, 162
Size, japan gold, 12, 32, 185, 193, 194
Size, parchment, 84
Sizing in, 62
Slapping in, 62
Soap, 28, 95, 102, 127, 162, 163, 196
Soap, Brooke's, 127
Soap for staining wicker work, 28
Soap, monkey, 102
Soapstone, 194
Soda, 29, 95, 96, 103, 107, 110, 154, 162, 178, 187
Soda, cracking as the result of using too much, 103
Soft woods, 9

Spanish mahogany, 9, 35, 88
Specks on varnished work, 177
Spindles, polishing, 121
Spirit black, 129
Spirit blue, 129
Spirit, coal-tar, 153, 154, 155
Spirit enamelling, 83
Spirit enamelling, colours for, 84
Spirit enamels, 172, 197
Spirit, methylated, 48, 55, 59, 61, 77, 82, 84, 85, 93, 102, 104, 105, 110, 111, 115, 118, 120, 122, 127, 129, 131, 150, 153, 156, 179, 183, 185, 186, 187, 188, 189, 190, 191, 193, 195, 197
Spirit rubber, 71
Spirit staining, 4
Spirit stains, 7
Spirit stains (*see* Recipes).
Spirit varnish, 108, 116, 148, 149, 156, 158, 171
Spirit varnish, brushes for, 172
Spirit varnish fillers, 59
Spirit varnish for dressing wood, 12
Spirit varnish for fretted articles, 172
Spirit varnish, removing, 96
Spirit varnishes, 156
Spirit varnishes, recipes for, 195, 196
Spirit varnishing, 171
Spiriting, 70
Spiriting pad, 71
Spirits of wine (*see* Alcohol).
Sponge, 170
Spruce, 9
Stained oaks (*see* Oak and its various finishes).
Stained polish for matching, 89
Stained woods (*see* Dyeing Woods and Impregnated Woods).
Staining, 15—38 (*see also* Stains).
 aim of, 1
 bleaching dark patches, 25
 brushes for, 17, 18, 19, 20
 brushwork, 15
 chemical, 4

212

Index

Staining—*contd.*
  classes of, 2
  colour chart for, 20
  colour schemes in, 22, 23
  coloured effects in, 147—150
  darkeners for, 25
  dressing wood for, 12
  ebonising, 26, 27
  fillers for, 13
  finishing off, 37
  floor margins, 37, 38
  knotting for, 18
  matching, 25
  oil, 4
  ornamental wood, 143, 147—150 (*see also* Ornamental Wood Staining).
  panels, 15, 16
  puttying before, 14
  relief material, 23
  soap used for wicker work, 28
  spirit, 4
  treatment of various woods, 31
  water, 3
  what it is, 1
  wicker work, 28
  wiping out, 23
  woods for, 9
Stains, black, 27, 28
  blended, 150
  blue, 29, 186
  cheapest kind, 5, 6
  chemical, 7
  ebony, 26, 27
  for floors, 37, 38
  for wax stopping, 53
  French black, 27, 28
  fumed oak, 129
  Johnson's, 6, 129
  Manders', 6
  oak, 33
  oil, 4, 7
  on polished work (ink, etc.), 109
  patent, 7, 8
  recipes for, 183—188
  rosewood, 33
  spirit, 7

Stains—*contd.*
  Stephens', 6, 7
  turpentine, 4, 5
  varnish, 7
  walnut, 34
  water, 5, 6
  wax, 4
  wicker work, blue, 29
    brown, 29
    golden yellow, 29
    green, 29
    red, 29
    violet, 29
Stains, recipes for, 183—188
Stationery cabinet with marquetry transfer, 132
Stencil brush, 143
Stencil, cutting a, 144
Stencil knives, 145, 146
Stencil plate, 144
Stencilling, blended stains on, 150
Stencilling on wood, 143—147
Stencils, 143—147
Stephens' fumed oak stain, 129
Stephens' stains, 6, 7
Stick lac, 39
Stiffing-up, 71, 72
Stippler, 19, 20
Stippling, 19
Stopping, coloured sticks of, 52
Stopping, hard, 14, 52
Stopping holes before polishing, 52
Stopping, wax, 52
Stopping, wax, how to use, 53
Stopping, wax, stains for, 53
Streakiness on varnished work, 177
Streaks, white, on polished work, 108
Subacetate of copper, 7
Sugar of lead, 195
Sulphate of iron, 7, 25, 185
Sulphuric acid, 72, 186, 196
Supporting work for polishing, 73—76
Swab, 102
Swab rubber for glazing, 79
Sweating on polished work, 101

Index

Sweating, reviver for, 102
Sweet oil, 88, 178
Sycamore, 9, 25, 27, 29, 34, 54, 61, 194
Sycamore, filler for, 149
Sycamore, staining, 34

TABLE, polishing Sheraton inlaid, 115
Tallow, 32, 33
Tallow, Russian, 33, 56
Tar, coal-, naphtha, 130
Tar, coal-, spirit, 153, 154, 155
Teak, 9, 56
Temperature for varnishing, 166
Temperature of polishing room, 43
Terebine, 178, 184, 185
Terra vert, 6
Testing varnishes, 179
Thuya wood, 9
Ties in stencils, 143—147
Tiger wood, 9
Timber (see Woods).
Tin, 29
Tin, airtight, for rubbers, 48, 64
Tool handles, polishing, 121
Tools (see Brushes).
Toppings, 72
Toys, varnish for, recipe, 197
Tragacanth, 61, 191
Transfer (marquetry), stationery cabinet with, 132
Transfers, marquetry, 119
Transparent varnish, recipe for, 196
Transparent white polish, 115, 190
Turmeric, 7, 185, 187, 188
Turned work, dull-polishing, 82
Turned work, polishing, 121
Turned work, supporting, 73, 74
Turpentine, 12, 32, 37, 38, 55, 56, 57, 89, 97, 108, 109, 115, 118, 122, 129, 134, 135, 137, 153, 154, 155, 156, 162, 174, 179, 180, 184, 185, 186, 193, 194, 195, 196, 197
Turpentine, American, 195

Turpentine and beeswax for wax-polishing, 137
Turpentine, good, 155
Turpentine stains, 4, 5
Turpentine, Venice, 84, 137

ULTRAMARINE, 187
Umber (see Burnt Umber and Raw Umber).
Umber, 24
Umber, brown, 56
Umbers, 7
Undercoats in varnishing, 180
Upholstered furniture, preparing for polishing, 50

VANDYKE brown, 6, 19, 33, 69, 89, 90, 91, 96, 97, 116, 118, 127, 128, 162, 184, 187, 194
Varnish, 151—181
 and polish fillers, 59
 applying, 168
 best quality, 153
 bottling and dating, 153
 brushes, 163, 164, 165, 172
 carriage, 153, 157
 church oak, 157
 Church seat, 159
 classes of, 156
 Coburg, 157
 Coburg and copal, 32
 copal, 32, 110, 157, 174, 180, 195
 colourless, 84
 dark, 157
 elastic and hard, 158, 159
 fillers, 59
 flatting, 174
 French oil, 157
 golden, 155
 hard, 157
 hard and elastic, 158, 159
 ingredients of, 152, 153
 light and dark, 157
 light for hardening, 180
 linseed oil for, 154
 lower class, 153
 making, 154
 maple, 157
 marble, white, 157

Index

Varnish—*contd.*
  mastic, 157, 196
  medium, 157
  mixtures, 180
  modern, 151
  naphtha, 131, 157
  natural, 158
  oak, 157
  oil, 157, 158
  oil, for dressing wood, 13
  paintings and pictures, for, 157
  pale, 157
  perfumed, recipe for, 197
  recipes for, 195, 196, 197
  removers, 94, 95
  removing old, 94
  removing spirit, 96
  selecting, 181
  shellac (knotting), 146
  spirit, 108, 116, 148, 149, 156, 158, 171
  spirit, for dressing wood, 12
  spirit, recipes for, 195, 196
  stains, 7
  straining, 181
  testing, 179
  to resist boiling water, 155
  toys, for (recipe), 197
  turpentine for, 155
  uses of, 152
  vessels for, 166
  violins, for, 155
  wallpapers, prints and maps, for, 157
  water, 156
  water, recipes for, 196, 197
  what it is, 151
  white, 157
  white hard, 150
Varnished, oil-, work, 104
Varnishing, 151—181
  application, 168
  blistering, 176
  bloom, 166, 175
  church seats, 159
  cissing, 170, 176
  cracking, 176
  creeping and crinking, 177
  curdling, 178

Varnishing—*contd.*
  double coating, 181
  dry, failure to, 178
  dull surfaces, 178
  dust, 167
  dusting, 168
  faults in, and their remedies, 175—179
  felting down, 169, 170
  finger marks, 178
  flaking, 177
  floor margins, 173
  fretted articles, 172
  general hints on, 180, 181
  grittiness, 177
  hints on, general, 180, 181
  light for, 180
  lustre, loss of, 177
  mixtures, 180
  new wood, 161
  outdoor work, 174
  painted work, 162
  patches, faulty, 175
  peeling, 177
  perishing, 177
  pinholding, 176
  pock marks and pitting, 176
  revarnishing, 163
  ropey surface, 178
  specks, 177
  spirit, 171
  streakiness, 177
  temperature whilst, 166
  undercoats, 180
  uniformity in, 180
  wrinkles, 177
Vegetable black, 69, 89, 127
Veins in woods, putting in, 91
Veneer (*see also* Inlay Work and Marquetry).
Veneered work, polishing, 113
Veneered work, removing blisters, 99
Veneered work, removing dents, scratches and burns, 100
Veneered work, repairing, 99
Veneers, dyeing, 29
Veneers, grain in, 118
Venetian red, 7, 38, 56, 89, 116, 118, 131, 183, 184, 186, 193

Index

Venice turpentine, 84, 137
Verdigris, 27, 185, 187
Vermilion, 187, 188
Vermilionette, 188
Vert terra, 6
Vessels for varnish, 166
Vienna chalk, 72
Vinegar, 21, 34, 95, 102, 108, 109, 127, 128, 179, 185, 186, 187, 192
Vinegar as a mordant, 21
Violet, methyl, 29
Violet stain, 29
Violins, varnish for, 155
Vitriol, Roman, 7

WAD (see RUBBER).
Wad rubber for fretwork polishing, 123
Wadding, 44, 45
Wadding, cotton, 43
Wallpapers, varnish for, 157
Walnut (see also Satin Walnut).
Walnut, 24, 31, 35, 36, 54, 56, 89, 116, 117, 118, 184, 194
Walnut, American whitewood for imitating, 31
Walnut, burr, 118
Walnut filler, recipe for, 194
Walnut, Italian, 9, 36
Walnut stain, 34
Walnut stains, recipes for, 184
Walnut, treatment of, 36
Washing before revarnishing, 163
Washing furniture, 98
Water, boiling, varnish to resist, 155
Water coating, 4, 7
Water coating, recipes for, 186
Water, lime, 102
Water marks on polished work, 110
Water staining, 3
Water stains, 5, 6
Water stains (see Recipes).
Water varnishes, 156
Water varnishes, recipes for, 196
Waterproof polish, 111
Waterproof varnish, recipe for, 196

Wax and resin, 139
Wax, Johnson's, 192
Wax, paraffin, 148
Wax-polish, ingredients of, 137
Wax-polish, preparing, 138
Wax-polished surfaces, renovating, 142
Wax-polishing, 137—142
Wax-polishing floors, 142
Wax-polishing, rubbers for, 140
Wax, powdered, 137
Wax, repairing woodwork with, 100
Wax stains, 4
Wax stopping, 52
Wax stopping, how to use, 53
Wax stopping, stains for, 53
Wax, white, 174, 196
Wax, yellow and white, 52, 137
White chestnut, 9, 116
White, flake, 84
White hard varnish, 150, 157
White marks on polished work, 108
White polish, 32, 61, 115, 190
White shellac, 40, 130
White wax, 174
Whitewood, 9, 10, 31, 56, 116
Whitewood, American, 9, 10, 31, 56, 183
Whitewood, American, for staining, 31, 183
Whitewood, American, stains for (recipes), 183
Whiting, 43, 56, 57, 84, 108, 115, 118, 122, 149, 185, 186, 187, 193, 194
Whiting, dry, 122
Wicker work, coloured stains for, 29
Wicker work, staining, 28
Wiping out in staining, 23
Woad, 186
Wood, dressing, 12, 13
Wood fillers for polishing, 54, 55
Wood, glass-papering, 11
Wood, impregnated, 25
Wood, improperly seasoned, 103
Wood, naphtha, 131, 153

Index

Wood, new, preparing for polishing, 51
Wood, preparing the, 10, 49
Wood, removing grease marks from, 11
Wood shavings for turned work, 121
Wood staining, ornamental, 143, 147—150 (*see also* Ornamental Wood Staining).
Wood, stencilling on, 143—147
Wood, varnishing new, 161
Woodcarving (*see* Carved work).
Woods :—
  alderwood, 25
  amboyna, 9, 56
  American whitewood, 9, 10, 31, 56, 183
  apple, 9, 27
  ash, 9, 54, 56, 61, 193
  basswood, 10
  baywood, 34, 88, 183
  beech, 9, 29, 193
  birch, 9, 25, 32, 54, 56, 183, 193
  birch, American, 9
  boxwood, 9
  Californian redwood, 9
  canary, 9, 10, 56, 183 (*see* American whitewood).
  canoe wood, 31
  cedar, 9
  cherry, 9, 27, 29, 193
  chestnut, white, 9, 116, 193
  cottonwood, 10
  deal, white, 9
  deal, yellow, 9
  ebony, 9, 56, 193
  elm, 54, 56, 194
  fir, red, Scotch and white, 9
  greenheart, 9
  hazelwood, 10
  holly, 9, 27, 29, 61
  hornbeam, 25
  Italian walnut, 9, 36
  jasper, 9
  lacewood, 9
  lime, 9
  magnolia, 31

Woods—*contd.*
  mahogany, 10, 24, 29, 31, 54, 56, 62, 88, 89, 115, 137, 183, 194
  mahogany, bay, 34, 88, 183
  mahogany, Cuban, 34
  mahogany, Honduras, 35, 88
  mahogany, Spanish, 9, 35, 88
  maple, 9, 54, 56, 116
  maple, bird's eye, 118, 194
  oak, 9, 10, 24, 54, 56, 61, 64, 83, 89, 91, 96, 97, 116, 117, 118, 125—132, 137, 148, 184, 194
  oak, American, 54, 129, 131
  oak, Indiana, 131
  olive, 9
  orange, 9
  padouk, 116, 117, 118
  pear, 9, 24, 27
  pine, 9, 24, 31, 32, 183, 194
  pine, Canadian, 9
  pine, canary, 31
  pine, kauri, 9, 31
  pine, northern, 9
  pine, pitch, 9, 24, 32
  pine, yellow, 9
  pitch pine, 9, 24, 32
  plane, 9
  plum, 24
  poplar, 9, 31
  rosewood, 9, 31, 35, 36, 54, 56, 184
  saddletree, 31
  satinwood, 9, 54, 56, 115
  satin walnut, 9, 33, 61, 64, 116, 194
  sequoia, 9
  spruce, 9
  sycamore, 9, 25, 27, 29, 34, 54, 61, 194
  teak, 9, 56
  thuya-wood, 9
  tiger-wood, 9
  walnut, 24, 31, 35, 36, 54, 56, 89, 116, 117, 118, 184, 194
  walnut, burr, 118

Index

Woods—*contd.*
    walnut, Italian, 9, 36
    walnut, satin (*see* Satin walnut).
    whitewood, 9, 10, 31, 56, 116
    whitewood, American, 10, 31, 56, 183
    white chestnut, 9, 116
    zebra, 9
Woods and veneers, dyeing, 29
Woods, characteristics of, 9
Woods, close-grained, 54, 68
Woods for dyeing, 29
Woods for ebonising, 27
Woods for staining, 9
Woods, hard, 9
Woods, mottled, 91
Woods, new, wax-polishing, 140
Woods, oil-polishing open-grained, 135
Woods, open-grained, 54, 68
Woods, soft, 9
Woods, stained (*see* Dyeing woods and Impregnated woods).

Woods, treatment of various, 31
Woodwork, cleaning old, 97, 98
Woodwork, outdoor, 174
Woodwork, repairing chipped, 100
Woodwork, washing, 98
Working up, 65
Workshop, the polishing, 42
Wrinkles on varnished work, 177

YELLOW arsenic, 187
Yellow, chrome, 129
Yellow lake, 6
Yellow, naphthaline, 29
Yellow ochre, 32, 33, 56, 89, 90
Yellow polish, 96, 97
Yellow resin, 84
Yellow stain, golden, 29
Yellow stains (self-colours), recipes for, 188
Yellow wax, 52

ZEBRA wood, 9
Zinc for stencils, 144

CPSIA information can be obtained at www.ICGtesting.com
Printed in the USA
LVOW060829290911

248261LV00005B/39/A